TEAM YOU

Awaken Clarity, Confidence, and Joy

by Honoring All Parts of Yourself

JEANINE CERUNDOLO

ISBN (ebook) 978-1-7370266-0-0
ISBN (paperback) 978-1-7370266-1-7

First Edition, 2021
Printed in the United States of America

Cover Design by Jelena Mirkovic
Interior Design by Jazmin Welch (fleck creative studio)
Typesetting by Sara Jane Filippini for fleck creative studio

Disclaimer and FTC Notice
Though this book is designed to provide information and motivation to readers, the purchaser or reader of this publication assumes responsibility for the use of these materials and information. Neither the publisher nor the author shall be liable for any physical, psychological, emotional, financial, or commercial damages, including, but not limited to special, incidental, consequential, or other damages. This publication is meant as a source of valuable information for the reader; however, it is not meant as a substitute for direct expert assistance. The advice and strategies contained herein may not be suitable for your situation. You should consult a professional where appropriate.

"With that Moon Language" from the Penguin publication *Love Poems From God: Twelve Sacred Voices from the East and West* by Daniel Ladinsky, copyright 2002 and used with permission.

Note: any hyperlinks in the text may be rendered obsolete over time.

PRAISE FOR *TEAM YOU*

"I started reading this book not really knowing what to expect. It intrigued me as I never heard of parts work. I instantly fell in love with the content and how Jeanine creatively guides the reader through deep inner work using parts mapping, journaling, meditation, and more. The exercises are challenging yet fun to work through as I discovered things about myself that I had unknowingly suppressed. This was a 'self-help' experience that I didn't know I needed."

— LAUREN CAP, YOGA TEACHER, NY

"With *Team You,* Jeanine has carefully crafted a powerful guide to connect readers with their inner selves through parts work in a way that is both gentle and encouraging. Through the coaching, activities, and examples in each chapter, I was able to get in touch with the needs and dynamics of my inner parts in a way that led to a much deeper understanding of how ignoring these in the past has created barriers to reaching my goals. More importantly, the book helped me to work with these parts in a holistic way that embraced them gently and allowed them to better communicate their needs in order to integrate them into my higher self. I am so grateful to have *Team You* as a vital resource and toolkit in my regular self-improvement practices."

— PHILIP JOHNSON, CAREGIVER, MN

"While most self-help books offer one-size-fits-all approaches, T*eam You* reveals how to connect with your own internal compass and blaze a tailored path to your best life. Jeanine's writing style is at once disarming and encouraging as she guides the reader to adopt tools that address barriers to behavior changes head on. Personally, it was very helpful to have this book as a resource while navigating once of life's biggest decisions—when and whether to start a family. Parts work helped me find a path forward from a divided mindset to a choice that brought peace."

— CHRISTINE DIVEN, PR & MARKETING, VA

"What a wonderfully refreshing and well-written self-help book! Jeanine exudes creativity and joy in her writing. I love the strategies to dig deep and get to know each individual piece of myself. Through using the tools in this book, I began to make decisions with greater ease and compassion. I feel so grateful and forever changed after reading Jeanine's work. This is a must-read for anyone in search of peace, clarity, and insight into their own mind!"

— SYDNEY DOOLITTLE, BREATH-WORK AND
AYURVEDIC PRACTITIONER, WY

"*Team You* could not have come at a better time. After a year where I lost both my parents, sold my first business and launched another, and gave birth to a second child, I found myself exhausted, scattered and coming apart at the seams. *Team You* helped me realize that coming apart was naturally what I was supposed to do. Through Jeanine's graceful guidance, I discovered insights, perspective and the exercises I needed to step out of life's swirl and into the eye of my existence. Her simple, but profound process took me to a place where I stopped serving—and started observing—the parts of me that were clamoring to be seen and heard. It helped me focus on nurturing new areas of growth, let go of old attachments, take the turmoil of transition and refocus it into a whole new level of transformation. I am grateful to Jeanine for the wonderful gifts she helped me unearth through the power of this book."

— PATRICK CONREAUX, MARKETING AND
CREATIVE LEADER, GA

"*Team You* delivers readers an accessible, practical, and step-by-step guide to uncover and befriend their parts so as to unlock the wisdom of their inner landscapes. This book is chock-full of innovative and expressive ways to contact and work with these parts of ourselves. It lays a strong foundation for cultivating true self-compassion, and provides practical methods for working through inner conflict. I am delighted and grateful for this beautiful offering representing a decade of internal and external work that Jeanine is gifting to the world. May you receive and relish the gift of *Team You!*"

— KATIE ASMUS, MA, LPC, BMP, THERAPIST AND MENTOR, CO

DEDICATION FROM THE AUTHOR

To you, the inner space explorer, the open-hearted one:

Thank you for being here.
Thank you for showing up.
Thank you for saying "Yes" to a process
that may both scare you and delight you.

Today, meet your fears and let them teach you.
Tune into your dreams and let them direct you.
Dare to trust that the messiness within you contains valuable messages.
Rest in the belief that what is scared in you is protecting what is sacred
in you.

Open to both the highest and the deepest versions of yourself.
There are parts of yourself you have hidden: Reveal them.
Parts you feel ashamed of: Love them.
Parts you put on a pedestal: See them for who they truly are.
Parts you cling to: Free them.
Parts you shun: Invite them in.

With a soft heart and a strong spirit, embrace all of you.

Thank you for dancing the dance,
for walking the walk,
And for taking a chance . . .

TABLE OF CONTENTS

INTRODUCTION

Have you ever felt a part of you wants to do one thing, but another part of you wants to do the exact opposite? In everyday conversation, we say things such as, "A part of me wants to go out with my friends, but another part of me just wants to stay home after such a long day!" Or we may think, "A big part of me really wants to get up early and go to the gym before work, but another part of me keeps hitting snooze every morning!"

When two sides of us are at odds, how do we know which way to turn or how to follow through with what we say is important? When facing a decision, either large or small, we may feel torn and frustrated, disagreeing with ourselves from the inside. We might feel even more confused by our "pros" and "cons" lists, which create a game of internal ping-pong.

In this book, you will explore the many different inner parts at play in your life—all the facets that make up you. You will learn to work with them so you can shift from inner conflict toward greater harmony. You will cultivate awareness and curiosity toward these parts, coming to understand them better. Rather than getting stuck in battles inside your mind, your internal dialogue will become more unified and support you in achieving your aims.

WHO THIS BOOK IS FOR

The pages that follow are a guidebook designed to support you in navigating the next steps in your life.

You are in the right place if:

> You are at a fork in the road and feel conflicted about which direction to choose.

> You fear taking a wrong turn and deviating from the path you believe you are "supposed" to be following.

> You are excited about the idea of having a greater purpose in your life or pursuing a passion, yet you are concerned about the practicalities of doing something new and out of the norm.

> You are in a transition with work, home, or relationships and feeling many things at once, such as disappointment, relief, grief, and hope.

> You have trouble making decisions. You often feel overwhelmed and paralyzed by the number of opportunities ahead, afraid to miss out on something.

> You are harder on yourself than anyone you know and cannot seem to break free from your self-admonishment.

> You have inspiring visions and dreams, but you hold yourself back and keep getting in your own way.

> You are interested in personal growth, spirituality, and developing your self-awareness.

> You are open-minded and curious to learn more!

With the tools offered here, you will learn how to move from inner division to inner peace.

HOW I WAS INTRODUCED TO PARTS

I first learned about working with parts from Katie Asmus, a dedicated and highly skilled mentor, therapist, and life coach I met in Colorado before I began my practice as a holistic life coach in 2012. In the few sessions we did together before I moved to New York City, Katie explained that she worked with a system[1] positing that we have 9-20 internal parts that are active inside of us. In the homework in between sessions, she prompted me to list these parts and describe each one. Becoming familiar with the idea of these internal parts through her guidance generated greater clarity and self-connection.

It is not uncommon in spiritually-oriented or therapeutic circles to hear people refer to comforting their inner child, consulting their inner mentor, or healing a wounded part. Thinking of the psyche as being comprised of parts was incredibly supportive in helping me get to know myself on many levels. This framework was a tool I could use to resolve the dissonance I felt when difficulties arose. Working with parts also gave me a way to listen to all sides of myself with loving and patient curiosity. Instead of resisting what was arising in me—which always made things worse—I could embrace my inner space with open-mindedness and understanding. In the years to follow, I applied these foundational insights to my life and in my work with clients.

In 2015, I began a master's program in Clinical Psychology at Teachers College, Columbia University. In my master's thesis, I explored the origins of "parts work" (as it is often called). Since then, I have also attended a seminar with Richard Schwartz, the founder of this work's most comprehensive model—Internal Family Systems (IFS). IFS is a rich methodology that has offered healing to thousands of clients, originally through therapy.

---

1   Katie Asmus's work was inspired by the "Self, Soul, Spirit" model, developed by her mentor, Roger Strachan.

I was stunned by how much overlap there was in that system with what I had been experiencing and was eager to deepen my learning. As I studied further, I developed a more nuanced approach to my own work with parts and connected with a community that was similarly enthusiastic about these tools. For further exploration, in the back of this book you will find a list of resources by Richard Schwartz and others.

The majority of my encounters with parts first took place in guided settings, either being guided by a therapist/coach or making the work tangible for others through guided visualization. This book will offer key lessons and illustrative anecdotes from what I have experienced and facilitated. My intention is to share these in an accessible format so that you can begin to apply and utilize these tools independently.

THE PURPOSE OF WORKING WITH PARTS

Working with parts can help you to feel more whole, be more forgiving of yourself and others, and experience greater compassion in your relationships. It can also help give direction with big choices such as moving far away, navigating career changes, becoming a parent, or stepping into your next chapter.

My clients have found the implementation of parts work very useful to inspire positive change in many situations and life transitions, including:

› Moving across the country with confidence instead of trepidation.

› Finding an inspiring dream job after years of burn-out at work.

› Healing from heartbreak and cultivating greater self-love.

› Deepening the flow of love through opening to a new romantic relationship.

› Generating greater wealth and creating increased impact through their work.

› Soothing worry, stress, and inner tension to make space for increased hope, vitality, and possibility.

› Gaining flexibility and fortitude when facing inevitable twists and turns.

› Renewing a sense of ease, connection, and flow in the unfolding of life events.

› Enjoying a sense of belonging through coming home to one's own being.

It can waste precious time, energy, and resources to be tormented by the conflict and self-criticism that wage war within you. Understanding yourself in terms of parts can shed light on the sides of you that are pitted against each other in staunch, sometimes even silent, opposition.

In this book, we will discuss how to give these parts a space to voice their needs, fears, and desires. The process of interacting with your parts will allow you to relate to yourself from a place of greater self-acceptance. From this place, all your parts can work together toward your highest good on the same team: *Team You!*

THE INTENTION OF *TEAM YOU*

In this book, you will learn to embrace the underlying value in all parts of yourself. The resulting stance of wholeness can lead to both healing and growth in multiple areas of your life. We will explore how to bring your parts to life through an engaging process so you can get to know them better. When you distinguish your parts and see them as individuals, you begin to understand your inner workings more fully.

You can gain insights and develop constructive beliefs that will help you make decisions from a centered place.

No part should single-handedly be behind the steering wheel of your life. Usually, we unconsciously let the loudest part run the show even though often this part is not in touch with the whole story. Rather than having one dominant part take over, your decisions and thought processes can reflect the integration of all your parts. When you make room for all aspects of yourself rather than overriding any one of them, they then have a chance to reveal their greatest gifts. With all of them on board, your inner team will become far more effective and calibrated to your true north.

Relating with your parts can therefore help you relate more harmoniously to yourself, the world, and your place in it. In developing a relationship with these parts, they can more easily get on board with behaviors that support your overall well-being instead of running rogue inside you.

As you explore your inner landscape, you can reduce the time you spend caught up in self-sabotage. Creating this consensus within helps you to feel less lost and more confident in being led by inner truth rather than torn by inner division. By getting in touch with your inner resources, you can experience increased compassion toward yourself and others as you move forward in life.

When we work with parts, we do not simply employ the imagination to create something from nothing; rather, the process evokes a recognition of what is already there. Representing your parts shines a light on your internal psychic components, ones that evolve as they reveal themselves. By relating to your inner space in this receptive way, you can better understand your inner workings and benefit from the transformation that can follow.

By the end of reading this book, you will likely think differently about the conversations you are having in your head. You will walk away with a new awareness of many of the possible parts within you, which will enable you to deepen your relationships with them—and thus with your whole self. Working closely with your parts can inspire you to thrive, finding fulfillment in what you do and in who you choose to be.

A NOTE ABOUT
THE SCOPE OF THIS BOOK

As a holistic life coach, I have been working with individuals and groups for years and am fascinated by the intricate workings of the human mind and heart. Since I am a life coach and not a therapist, a word here on the difference is in order. While it is true that the work overlaps in certain aspects, they are also distinct in several ways.

First, therapy and coaching can be seen as different in their aims. Therapy is the modality best suited for promoting healing in clinical situations, such as recovering from psychological pain or past trauma. It can be seen as analogous to getting physical therapy for a wound such as a broken ankle. On the other hand, coaching entails a process of "leveling up" from a resourced starting point, akin to training to run a marathon when you already have a solid foundation. Coaching thus often focuses on shepherding future-oriented personal or professional goals to the next phase of their actualization. At the same time, coaches must also know how to address any blocks to the client's growth and navigate limiting beliefs or sticking points that have become patterns.

Coaching and therapy both share an intention to help clients overcome their inner obstacles and thrive. These two modalities share some similar tools and place central importance on cultivating a supportive client-practitioner alliance. Practitioners in either discipline can take a more goal-oriented or process-oriented approach as they companion clients on their journey of self-discovery. Ultimately, both coaches and therapists facilitate a process of helping the client connect with their core essence and become free to align with and express more of who they truly are.

Some practitioners versed in therapy and coaching use parts work in both modalities but emphasize different things depending on what the client needs. Katie Asmus, the therapist and coach who first introduced me to parts work, explained that she uses this method in therapy to help heal wounded parts. In those cases, the externalization of the parts helps ground people and avoids a downward spiral of intensely pained parts. That approach allows the client to adopt a witnessing stance and not blend with the parts inside them that are suffering. Katie also makes sure to bring forth parts that elicit supportive inner resources to bolster the person's whole system—mind, body, heart, and spirit. In a coaching setting, she shifts her focus to applying parts work to enable a client to increase their self-awareness. By uncovering their drives, values, and needs, they gain greater self-confidence and clarity with decision-making.

In my coaching practice, I rely on parts work when needed but not as the totality of what I offer. If my coaching kit is a toolbox, then parts work is like a wrench and is utilized when a wrench is most suitable. The coaching process offers many other tools, such as strategies from positive psychology, holistic techniques for setting intentions and reaching goals, and frameworks for inspiring personal development. I choose to bring parts work into the coaching conversation when I deem it will be the most effective way to facilitate insight and encourage growth. Usually, this is in cases where someone is stuck in inner conflict, grieving a loss, or experiencing a fear that is impeding forward motion.

There are many ways to work with your inner parts. My intention in sharing my experience with you is that you take what resonates with you and apply it to your struggles and aims. That said, this work is very powerful, and it can open the psyche in profound and challenging ways.

If you struggle with acute mental or emotional challenges, or if you uncover buried or sensitive parts that are deeply pained, parts work would be best explored through the lens of IFS. This therapeutic model addresses clinical issues such as addiction, trauma, self-harming tendencies, eating disorders, depression, and overwhelming anxiety, helping you connect with the parts of you that are involved in those experiences. The IFS tools can help someone navigate the healing journey regarding wounded or pained parts. Given the nature of my work and experience, this book will not cover aspects of parts work that are specific to therapy and thus cannot substitute for therapy. If it is an option, it can be very supportive to work with a trained parts work therapist or IFS counselor with a background in psychotherapy. You can also refer to the resource section of the book for writings that take a therapeutic approach to this work.

A last note in that regard: when we speak here of dialogue between different inner voices, we are not referring to Dissociative Identity Disorder (formerly called Multiple Personality Disorder). In that particular constitution, these parts have split in a more polarized way in the mind and body, usually triggered by trauma. In those situations, one might lose access to the interconnection between their parts and the awareness of their wholeness. In that case, exploring this work with the support of a licensed mental health counselor is advised, as the parts could display particular dynamics that require special treatment and care, at least initially.

A NOTE ON THE
STRUCTURE OF THIS BOOK

Psychologists have been exploring the parts of the psyche in different contexts for decades. The perspective offered in this book is derived from my graduate studies at Columbia University on parts work, as well as my personal and professional experience. I have also been a student of my own experience, using what arises as an opportunity to practice. Understanding the sides of me, working with them, and guiding this process for others has led to profound changes in my life and the lives of those with whom I have the honor of working. This book is intended as an introduction to the concept of inner parts so that you can have tools to start working with them on your own. It will also provide you with a starting point to working with a guide, if you are inspired to go deeper.

In each chapter, there are descriptions of my tailored process of connecting with parts, with anecdotal examples from clients with varied backgrounds (in terms of age, gender, sexual orientation, race, ethnicity, spiritual and faith traditions, and location). These client stories have been included with permission, though the examples are necessarily abridged, and names and identifiable details have been changed or omitted for privacy. At the end of each chapter, I provide prompts and practices for applying the themes and lessons of each chapter to your life and current situation.

In sharing my experience with this modality, I hope my journey—and those of my clients—help you to learn more about yourself and develop more kindness, gentleness, and care for all the parts of yourself.

Thank you for your willingness to explore your inner space through learning about these tools and concepts. I hope that after reading this book, you can look in the mirror of your many selves and kindly welcome all that you see.

Let's Dive In!

I.

GETTING TO
KNOW YOU(S)

Parts work is based on the premise that we have many parts inside ourselves, each with unique personalities, fears, hopes, wants, needs, desires, and histories. Our first step is simply awareness—familiarizing ourselves with this idea of parts and taking stock of which ones are impacting us the most.

With non-judgmental observation as our foundation, let's take an inventory of what your current parts are like and how they show up in your inner system.

CHAPTER 1:
WHAT ARE PARTS?

Learn to See Many Sides of Yourself

You are allowed to be both a masterpiece
and a work in progress, simultaneously.

— SOPHIA BUSH

One of the themes we will explore in this book is the balance between your inherent wholeness in the present and the newness of what is emerging within you as you seek to grow. You will learn how to embrace who you are now, even as you step into what comes next. Some aspects of yourself you might already willingly accept, and others you might be shunning. But all of the parts of you are here, and their inherent goodness is worth honoring.

THINKING OF "YOURSELF"
AS "YOURSELVES"

For many years, psychologists have explored this concept of psychic multiplicity—the notion that rather than being one singular whole inside our mind, we can relate to our human experience as one that is comprised of diverse aspects of ourselves. In this chapter, we will begin by getting familiar with the idea that the perception of an individual self can be viewed instead as a collection of selves. From this viewpoint, your decisions, behaviors, and emotions correspond to inner parts of yourself that are all deserving of your attention.

Moments in our lives often elicit different sides of ourselves; whether an apparent threat triggers a fearful part, a perceived criticism provokes a protector part, or a dazzling distraction tempts a playful part. For some, this seems intuitive and makes sense as soon as it is introduced. For others, it is novel and may feel intriguing, though not as natural. When you think of your internal landscape, do you find it easy or difficult to segment your conception of yourself into a variety of specific personas?

From a western psychological perspective, this notion of parts can be traced back to Carl Jung's work in the early 1900s in the Jungian concept of "archetypes and complexes." Since then, aspects of parts work have shown up in various forms across different therapeutic modalities. These include Gestalt Therapy, Ego State Therapy, Voice Dialogue, Psychosynthesis, Hypnotherapy, Psychodrama, and, most recently and comprehensively, the Internal Family Systems model developed by Richard Schwartz.

Much of the formal parts work to date was originally developed under the jurisdiction of therapy to address and help heal trauma. The practice of working with parts to heal and grow now has many derivations and applications. In many of these modalities, parts are sometimes called sub-personalities since each part can be as complex as a whole person. In this book, I will refer to your internal aspects as "parts," though thinking of them as entities of their own can help you deepen your relationship with them.

The processes in this book will help you crystallize the essence of your inner workings. By bringing mindfulness to the parts at play within yourself, you can untangle their individual automatic reactions from a more unified underlying truth. In the pages ahead, you will get to know—and then relate with—your parts so you can incorporate their gifts into the gift of who you are. By witnessing your inner workings, you can start to experience less confusion, discord, and internal conflict.

WHOLENESS INCLUDES ALL PARTS

When I was first introduced to the concept of parts, it made so much sense to me that I started applying it in my own life. My outgoing side was oriented toward making the most of life and enjoying life's precious gifts. At the same time, my introspective side was prone to being overwhelmed by periods of inexplicable sadness. Before encountering parts work, I was inclined to label those darker feelings as wrong or inconvenient. However, resisting them only caused me to deny a visceral and rich part of my inner experience and reality.

At some point, I heard a saying attributed to Carl Jung that has stuck with me since: "I would rather be whole than good." Sometimes, our concept of "being a good person" involves conforming to an unrealistic idea of perfection. When we strive to align with a limited concept of what is acceptable, we may cut ourselves off from any truth that does not meet those criteria. In trying to prove our own goodness to ourselves, we might cast anything outside of our ideal into the shadows. By fixating on a romanticized self-identity and denying parts of ourselves that we deem less likable, we leave little room to embrace the fullness of our humanity. A holistic experience of life includes low points, tears, anger, confusion, messiness, and complexity. Carl Jung's quote emphasized for me that an experience of being human that includes all our parts is preferable to (and truer than!) one that stunts our authenticity and genuine expression.

In the mainstream, we can also see these concepts of parts, integration, and wholeness beautifully illustrated in the animated Pixar film *Inside Out* (2015). In the movie, the protagonist Riley moves across the country with her family, leaving behind her childhood home—and her childhood—as she starts to become a young woman. What makes this movie unique is that it is told from the perspective of her emotions. The five characters of Joy, Sadness, Anger, Disgust, and Fear operate the control panels of Riley's brain. What happens among them dictates her perception, choices, memories, and ultimately her future.

Sadness, who is ever unappreciated, is introduced derogatorily by Joy, who remarks, "I'm not actually sure what she does. And I've checked, there's no place for her to go, so . . . " Throughout most of the movie, Sadness feels out of place and like a burden to Joy, and even to Riley. Sadness spends much time moping around in her own feelings of shame and a low sense of self-worth.

However, Sadness does end up finding her place, quite by accident. In fact, she arguably becomes the heroine of the movie when she displays her surprising superpower. In a poignant scene, Joy and Sadness are lost within Riley's memory bank. They desperately need the help of Riley's imaginary friend, Bing Bong, to lead them to a train back to the headquarters of Riley's mind, where they can do their vital jobs. However, along the way, Bing Bong begins to realize that his connection to Riley is fading. As Riley grows up and visits the fictional worlds of her younger days less and less, the threads that connected her to Bing Bong start to unravel. Bing Bong becomes teary at the idea of losing his relationship with Riley forever. Joy, ever driven, insists that they must leave and tries to distract him, cheer him up, and coax him to move, but all her efforts do not budge Bing Bong, who is paralyzed by his sorrow.

Sadness takes a radically different approach. She sits with Bing Bong and empathizes with him in his nostalgia, pain, and dismay, as she knows these feelings well. Once he has had the chance to be heard in his truth, Bing Bong finds relief and his despondency subsides. Comforted, he gets up to help them find the train, leaving Joy dumbfounded. "How did you do that?" Joy asks incredulously. "I don't know, he was sad, so I listened . . . " Sadness replies.

When we, too, can listen to ourselves and others from a place of compassion, we can move through what is arising with more grace. In the end, Sadness's role of revealing what is precious in Riley's life deepens Riley's connection to herself and her loved ones, helping her mature. Joy and the other emotions learn that Sadness is necessary because by being the one who allows Riley to grieve, Sadness's vulnerability makes space for Riley's loved ones to come closer and to comfort her. From there, Joy often follows naturally, and these two emotions even become dependent on each other and less black and white. Without Sadness, Riley would be numb and indifferent and might have even followed through with her plan to run away from the new house she despises. When Riley's sadness is expressed to her parents, they all admit they miss their old life and begin to bond as they form a new home together.

In this premise of *Inside Out*, we see vividly how our emotional landscape subconsciously influences our behaviors. We see how chaos can ensue when these internal drivers are disconnected from each other. The movie underscores the message that the richness of our human experience lies in connecting with *all* our emotions—and allowing them to connect with each other—rather than simply favoring one. In essence: to be true to ourselves, we must make room for both the light and the shadow.

Though *Inside Out* focuses on detailing inner parts in terms of emotions, you can work with parts that are more complex, each having their own unique personalities, fears, hopes, needs, desires, and histories. Some parts can be universal, like the archetypes of the inner child or the inner mentor. Others can be more specific and personal to you, like Darrell the Daring, who emerged on your bungee jumping adventure (which Percy the People Pleaser did *not* tell your mother about).

Most importantly, a foundational belief of this work is that even though we are works in progress, we are also whole just as we are. We are already worthy of acceptance and belonging. It is natural to feel like we need to get somewhere else or become someone else before that love is truly possible. However, in working with our parts, we can learn to embrace all aspects of ourselves—and let others see and love us for who we are, too. We can start to know ourselves as complete in this moment while we are also evolving and growing at the same time.

Let's consider the metaphor of the phases of a flower's growth. A flower, when bloomed, is utterly beautiful in its unfurled expression. It is exactly what it was meant to become. And yet, the bud is also perfect in its formation. We would not yell at a bud and say, "You are wrong to be a bud! You have to be a flower already! Hurry up and stop being so not-there-yet!" The tender bud is a flower in the making. It is on its own timeline, and the only thing that will help it flourish into a flower is nurturing it with the right doses of sunlight, water, good soil, and time.

At any given point in our lives, we are both the flower and the bud, simultaneously. You cannot force a bud open without hurting it. If you pried it open prematurely, you would harm it in your attempt to initiate progress before its time. Only by being nourished will a bud blossom into fruition. Likewise, rather than force yourself into changing, you can learn to lovingly accept yourself and surrender to the subsequent and natural transformation that follows.

This book is an invitation to embrace the parts of you that are fully blooming as well as the parts of you that are budding—or still seeds. As a tree grows, it can only spread its branches as high as its roots run deep. When we dare to go to the depths, we also enable ourselves to soar to our highest heights.

In the chapters to follow, each will end with a suggested activity to help you connect to both who you are and who you are becoming as you learn to embrace both at once. Today, we will explore one of your deepest desires as well as the daunting fears that have been keeping those very desires at bay.

CHAPTER 1 ACTIVITY:

Connect with your Dreams and Dragons

Let's tune in now to get a sense of what is present in your inner landscape. One of my clients remarked that she never knew what to expect from some of the homework I recommended until she actually sat down to do it. When she showed up attentively and put in the work, insights emerged that she had not anticipated. I encourage you to allow each chapter's activities to be something you engage with meaningfully, letting yourself get curious about what can unfold in your exploration.

Ready? Let's begin.

Take time to be relaxed as you do this activity. To go within, you can close your eyes; take long, deep breaths; make some tea; or play your favorite calming music.

Today's activity is designed to kickstart our process by activating some parts via a circumstance you are encountering in your life.

Today, begin by journaling via the prompts below. You may journal by hand, typing, or even via a recorded audio note.

1) YOUR DESIRES *(15 minutes)*

Reflect: What do you want most in your life? Describe what comes up in detail. How do you imagine you will feel if you obtain these outcomes?

These desires are connected to your deepest **dreams**. Even if they start as whispers, they matter. They are the doorway to your aliveness.

2) YOUR BLOCKS *(15 minutes)*

Internally, what tends to stop you the most? What inner barrier causes the biggest obstacle to achieving what you desire? How do you feel when that fear, bad habit, or limiting belief holds you back and gets in the way of your progress?

These are your **dragons**. They are the protective forces that imprison you "for your own good" out of fear that, if you leave your comfort zone, you may encounter some kind of harm in the process.

3) YOUR PARTS *(5 minutes)*

Notice any inner voices that pop up as you describe the aspirations you wrote about in response to Question 1. What do these voices tend to say? Do they caution you? Encourage you? Describe them. At first, this process could seem quite "out there," so keeping an open mind is very useful!

Note: The more you stoke the flames of your desires, connecting to those long-held (and potentially long-awaited) dreams, the louder and more ferocious your dragons can become in response. The level to which you seriously engage with actualizing what you truly want is often the level to which your fears will rise, starting to rear their heads and looming larger than before. They become on high alert for any scent of change, which is inherently alarming to these protectors. At least initially, they may strongly resist you "going for it," as it seems too wild! Once you work with those protectors to help them trust you (which we will do later in the book), they may not rebel as much in the face of such change.

Suggestion: As you are journaling, if you find it hard to conceive of any specific parts (whether they are dreamer-type parts or dragon-type parts), try rereading this chapter and notice what aspects of you are responding to the words here. When you have reactions pop up, ask, "Which part of me is thinking that?" See if you can identify a voice or two in there.

For example, if you read through an activity and think, "Yeah, right—I'm not going to do that!", which part of you is resisting the suggestion? What does that part look like? Sound like? What are they wearing? How old do they seem to be?

And if a part of you is saying, "Oh, wow! I've never thought about that before—I'm going to try it!" which part of you is *that*? What do *they* look like? Sound like? Act like?

If you cannot see or imagine any part like this so far, do not be alarmed—the part that may worry that you are doing it wrong is another part! Just keep reading and pay attention to what resonates and what might be a seed that could bear fruit in the future. Remember, this work is dynamic and will become easier with practice.

INTRODUCTION & CHAPTER 1
KEY CONCEPTS

> The mind can be seen as containing many selves or parts, rather than being a singular entity. Psychologists have been studying and exploring the idea of sub-personalities for decades in various forms.

> Parts can show up as inner archetypes (child, mentor, critic) or aspects of yourself that appear as specific inner characters (Joe the Jester, who was called a class clown by his teachers). In the Pixar movie *Inside Out*, Riley's parts were represented by her predominant emotions.

> By connecting with your parts in daily life, you can more gracefully navigate transitions, internal conflicts, and daunting fears.

> Working to understand and integrate your parts is called parts work. You can relate with your parts, which helps you receive their valuable messages and gifts.

> One of the most comprehensive models for working with parts is called Internal Family Systems. It was developed by Richard Schwartz, a family therapist who discovered that, intrapsychically, we have our own inner families.

> Therapy and life coaching overlap but are distinct in important ways. Simply put, therapy often focuses on healing, integrating, and confronting the past to restore wholeness, whereas coaching tends to place greater emphasis on fulfilling meaningful future goals. Ultimately, both help support people to cultivate wellness from the inside out.

> In this book, we will explore an introduction to your parts in the context of life coaching. We will generate inspired action toward

your goals in an approachable way by freeing you from your conflicted inner dialogue.

› In the pages ahead, you will begin to assemble the parts of you into an ultimate "inner team," which can support you in realizing both your deepest and highest aspirations.

› You are invited to adopt the perspective that you are already whole, complete, and good. It is when parts are ignored, denied, and avoided that you could become blind to the wisdom they might hold. By opening to what each part has to say, a return to wholeness can emerge.

› The activity in Chapter 1 will help get you in touch with a desire and a roadblock within your life. From there, you can start to tune in for any parts that might be active and noticeable when you consider your path ahead.

CHAPTER 2
IDENTIFYING YOUR PARTS

List Your Parts and Reveal Your Inner Aspects

Do I contradict myself?
Very well then I contradict myself,
(I am large, I contain multitudes.)

— WALT WHITMAN, *SONG OF MYSELF*

So far, we have focused on the first element in parts work: awareness. Now, we will continue with that theme by getting to meet some of your specific parts. By enumerating the ones you currently notice, you can unveil a fuller range of parts and get your first glimpse of this cast of internal players.

In this chapter, you will find sample lists of parts and some common roles they might play, as well as their motives, fears, and intentions. Identifying your parts is a valuable starting point in the process of working with them because in separating yourself from them, you gain an outside perspective. The space between "you" and any "part of you" is key to seeing what insights each has for you.

Through the activity in this chapter, we will take inventory of the facets of you at play, creating a sketch of your inner life from there. Though initially we will use emotions, roles, and archetypes as a doorway into a part, keep in mind that parts are not as fixed or exaggerated as they might initially appear. Different parts can come and go in the field of your awareness, and since they are dynamic, parts will likely shift as you get to know them. Like people, parts can hold multiple perspectives, feelings, and needs at once, so do not assume that the thread you first pull to identify them is the full story. Rather than pigeonhole any part into a particular stance or state of being, recognize their emotional range and capacity to transform.

Whatever you discover as your parts first appear will not be a final picture but just an introduction. As your parts express themselves more fully, you may find yourself thinking of them in a new light. These enhanced perceptions are emergent, especially as we explore the interrelationships among parts. For now, we will simply get to know them individually as they show up today.

MEETING YOUR INNER SELVES

When some people first hear about parts, they can find the idea a bit foreign. If you are feeling that way right now, that is okay! In my experience, once people begin working with their parts, the process becomes highly intuitive, and they can usually get right into the flow.

Most of the people with whom I work can connect with their parts by visualizing them. They perceive each part's style of clothing, countenance, and the emotional texture of their presence. Depending on what they represent in the moment, the parts can appear as personified aspects of oneself at different periods in time, such as a child self or a taller, older self. Some have even shown up as a shape-shifting blob, an animal, a creature, or as an element, such as an elusive or heavy fog. Some clients relate to parts in terms of where they feel them in their body, as an emotion or sensation, as colors, or in an auditory way. There is no wrong way to greet and get to know your parts. I work predominantly in the visual sphere, so I will refer to parts in this manner. If you connect to them in different ways, feel free to follow what arises and do what works best for you.

When you meet them, the parts can present themselves with specific attributes in terms of their appearance, such as dress, colors, posture, gender, age, etc. However, it is not necessary to know the possible meaning of these particularities. Without reading into what you perceive, you can still feel the significance of these details on a symbolic level. Parts work relies on your imagination and tunes into your intuition to access information of which you may be only subconsciously aware. The intuitive nature of working with parts is very much like following a lucid dream during which you are semi-awake and receptive. The process is fluid and amorphous yet can still evoke profound feelings.

In my work with clients, I found several common parts that are useful to consider at the start of our work together. Once the essence of these figures is introduced, clients tend to instinctively understand the energy of each and can describe them. I am always amazed at how similarly people depict their core parts. At the same time, each person's experience with their parts and interpretation of them is truly unique and creative.

Below, I have included descriptions of several archetypal parts that I have come across over the years. As you read, feel free to adapt the characteristics listed alongside each part to match the personal conception that you have of it.

Note: Parts can be any gender (or genderless) regardless of a person's overall gender identity. For simplicity, I will alternate using he and she in the descriptions that follow.

WISE ONE WITHIN/HIGHER SELF

As the truest and deepest version of yourself, this Wisdom Keeper can be thought of as a container for all your parts. Arguably, the goal of working with parts is to connect with this soulful and transcendent energy, often called your Higher Self or Inner Mentor. Sometimes the other parts are so noisy it is hard to hear the Wise One Within. The more you work with those parts and help them resolve their concerns, the more space you create to let this benevolent force lead. It is not practical to expect the Wise One Within to be at the helm at all times (I do not know about you, but I am not yet close to enlightenment!), but it is something you can orient toward by increasing your ability to bring her to the fore.

When The Wise One Within is invoked and accessed, this figure is often felt as a calm and comforting presence. She is your most resourced self, who can lovingly preside over the meeting of the other parts. She has depth and grounded guidance to offer, though she usually says few words. Instead, she compassionately holds the space with care. This Self is gentle, generous, kind, and knowing.

Your Wise One Within is the seat of your internal compass and graciously allows things to unfold, with reverence for the way things are. She sees the bigger picture and can thus be a moderator for parts in conflict. The Wise One Within can illuminate paths forward or offer approaches that you might not have considered.

Rather than worrying, the Wise One Within places faith in what she can act on, utilizing previously unseen resources to create more ease. The Wise One Within can appear as a serene version of you or even a historical figure, enlightened teacher, or personal mentor whose essence reassures you. The Wise One Within's soothing mantra may be something like, "You are loved, you are okay, and you already have your own answer." When you align with the energy of your Wise One

Within, you may feel a relaxed sense of grace and peace that both washes over you and emanates from you.

We will explore the Wise One Within more in-depth in Chapter 7.

INNER CHILD/CORE SELF

The Inner Child is the version of you that expressed itself freely in your youngest years, sometimes referred to as your Core Self. This pristine embodiment of your spirit is bright, joyful, delightful, and delighted. Usually visualized as a very small child (three to seven years old), this aspect precedes any internal or external harms that have befallen you in your life. The Inner Child's main objective is to be in the world and experience it with wonder and a sense of awe. This child is eternally bright and unconditionally open, simple, and warm. The harms or worries of life tend to roll off the back of this playful child who trusts in the best.

The Inner Child is not driven by fear or self-doubt but rather has an earnest self-assuredness and eagerness about him. He can show up as pure, wide-eyed, centered, and gleeful. Connecting with this endearing part often brings up fondness, sweetness, and tenderness. The Inner Child may not use many words but may show his feelings through gestures, gifts, or facial expressions. When you let the Inner Child live through you in the present as an adult, that may look like following your gifts freely, giving generously, trusting deeply, or having fun in a playful and relaxed way.

TEENAGE SELF/WOUNDED CHILD

This part is sometimes called the Wounded Child, as she has taken on the painful elements of life. The Teenage Self shoulders the hardships of betrayal, heartbreak, sorrow, and insecurity, often born from external experiences that she internalized. She can be the manifestation of hurt, forming at the first instance of intense pain or suffering in your life. The Teenage Self tends to be preteen or teenaged, or of the age when she first encountered deep sadness and experienced a loss of innocence.

The Teenager Self can appear despondent and dejected, as if life will always be filled with sorrow or challenge. She often is described as quiet, sullen, and tentative, looking at her feet. She can also have a rebellious tone, as she is starved for love, even if she tries to attain it in unhealthy ways. This child harbors a reservoir of pain and consequently is often skeptical of affection, as she has felt let down so often before.

When the Teenager Self feels disappointed and discouraged, her complaint might be something like, "What's the use? Nobody listens to me or understands. Things will never get better this way." Underneath this heavy sigh is a strong desire for change. She might bear the weight of the world's problems on her shoulders, feeling exhausted from thinking she is alone in her struggle to better her plight or trying to improve something unjust in the world around her. She usually can feel angry or withdrawn around adults but often softens when interacting with the younger Inner Child or any similarly innocent energy that trusts her.

The Teenage Self is usually a sensitive aspect of you who cares deeply about something precious but has not yet seen it fulfilled in her eyes and is starting to lose faith. The Teenage Self may also suffer from feeling stunted around channeling her gifts, not having found anyone to receive what she has to offer. When this part is loved and can take steps toward healing, she can use the very source of her former pain to give back meaningfully to others who have experienced the same thing.

See the "Resources" section at the back of this book for tools on working more in-depth with the wounded inner child, or refer to IFS work for their findings on exiles and burdens.

INNER CRITIC/CRITIC

This part may often come across as stern, rigid, bossy, intimidating, and harsh. Ultimately, the Inner Critic is behaving like this in a grand effort to keep you safe as his greatest fear is that you will fail, be rejected, or be otherwise harmed. This part is skeptical of you and your decisions. Underneath it all, the Inner Critic is trying to protect you but often does so through a lens of what-could-go-wrong, aiming to avoid that at all costs. Your Inner Critic might repress your creativity and expression by focusing only on coloring within the lines of his perceived limitations. He doubts your abilities and echoes your parents' or teachers' criticisms of you.

His mantra might be something like, "Be practical," "Don't rock the boat," or "Stay under the radar." He can compare you to others, saying things like, "Success in the arts is only for the lucky few, people much more talented than you!" Or, he may cut you down to size, sneering, "Who do *you* think you are to attempt to build a company on your own?" Your critical part may also generalize things, such as warning, "No one will like you if…" or "Everybody will laugh at you when…"

The Inner Critic can appear in a variety of forms. Some aspects related to this critical stance can be fearful, driven, or worried parts such as:

› **Scaredy Cat**

This fearful part is like a personification of the raw fear behind the Inner Critic's protective micro-management. The Scaredy Cat often appears first as a blob, an animal, or a sulky, down-trodden human form. This part is usually nervous, sometimes visualized as trembling, hiding, or caged when you first encounter it. It can feel ashamed, skittish, worried, and frightened of outcomes that, though unlikely, seem terribly daunting in its eyes. It may isolate itself in a corner or try to shrink itself to evade the vulnerability of being seen. Scaredy Cat's common thoughts may be along the lines of, "Don't attract attention. Be suspicious. Everyone is guilty until proven innocent (and even then . . .)." Sometimes, this part changes size and shape as it feels more or less safe. When healed, it usually reveals a precious part of you that previously felt uncomfortable showing and sharing itself.

› The Ambitious One/Potential Seeker

This highly driven part is geared toward success and obsessed with you reaching your potential. This part is stressed that you will not make a significant impact in the world, nor reach your goals. He is fueled by fear of not being "good enough" and seeks to earn the approval—or love—of others by proving himself worthy. He thinks you will operate best under stress and thus applies pressure, pushing ahead at a breakneck pace.

This Ambitious One is a go-getter who is constantly striving for greater heights or for something better. He may have unreasonable expectations of himself and others, feeling disappointed when his standards are not met. He is seldom satisfied, as he is convinced there is always more that can be achieved. When his ambitions are unintegrated or when this part attempts to run the show, the Ambitious One's tactics can be unsustainable. Since his ethos is "go-go-go," he views taking any breaks as lazy rather than essential. His rallying cry might be along the lines of, "It's not enough" or, "Make sure to make the **most** of life!"

The Ambitious One insists on maintaining a high gear as he believes it will make you outrun failure. He is willing to leave other things you care about in the dust in this quest. His pedal-to-the-metal approach may make you feel off-kilter and induce anxiety. In an integrated system, this part might incorporate an ability to accept progress over perfection and take on a role as a Motivating Leader or Strategic Advisor.

› **The Worry Wart**

The Worry Wart could be a manifestation of the Inner Critic that strives to beat negative situations to the punch by anticipating them in your own mind. He may worry about your physique and try to control your appearance; he may worry about hurting others or being hurt and counsel you to withdraw; he may try to give you a "reality check" when you want to explore something new and unknown. His concerns are often in stark contrast to—and fueled by—a Dreamer part's more lackadaisical ways. The Worry Wart sees his credo of caution as a matter of survival. When integrated, a worrying part can reveal what you care about and hold those concerns with an awareness free of unwarranted fear.

We will cover the Inner Critic more in-depth in Chapter 6 as it is often a familiar part, though nuanced.

MUSE/DREAMER

This inspiring and inspired part is often highly animated, creatively expressive, joyfully fun, and energetically idealistic. Hopeful, creative, and in love with possibility, the Muse enjoys letting her imagination run wild. Sometimes, the Muse comes onto a scene dancing, doing cartwheels, or grinning from ear to ear. The Muse wants you to go for it (whatever your particular "it" may be), and to follow your heart's desires. Her effusive enthusiasm is not limited by current realities and is as expansive as her vast imagination.

The Muse's mantras may be, "Live and make the most of things! Don't settle for a dull, boring life. Play! Have an adventure! Carpe Diem!"

Often, this part is larger-than-life and makes you smile. She tends to be as welcoming as the most gracious host and heartwarming in her approach to you. Though she often stimulates the worries of her counterpart, the Inner Critic, she tends to dismiss his gloom and doom. She much prefers to enjoy the moment or dream up a new plan that inspires her.

Other roles and archetypes related to the Muse could be: Inventor, Visionary, Pleasure-Seeker, Adventurer, or Optimist. These parts may either be very focused on enjoying the moment at the expense of thinking about the future or so inspired by the visions of the future that they abandon the concerns of the present. When integrated, they help you stay in touch with your aliveness while remaining connected to practical realities, thus becoming both grounded and encouraging.

—

Keeping some of these archetypes in mind, remember that everybody's parts are unique. It is a creative process to uncover which specific ones are key players for you today. You can use the list above as a starting point and let the process inform you as you go.

Let's look at a few examples to see how unique each person's approach to forming their lists can be.

ROBERT'S PARTS LIST AND IMPRESSIONS

When I first started working with Robert, I introduced him to a few of these most common characters through a guided visualization. He then spent some time expanding his inner team by writing about more parts that came to mind. I asked him to imagine each part as a person and to describe them as vividly as he could, including details such as apparent age, countenance, appearance, dress, and defining characteristics. This exercise was an opportunity for him to reflect in a free-form way on other aspects of his personhood.

Here is what he wrote:

PARTS WORK	AS THEY COME TO MIND...
HIGHER SELF	Harry: 45, tall and lean, well dressed, brown hair, calm and relaxed, soothing, knowing, gentle, wise, thinking and listening, intelligent, non-judgmental
CORE SELF	Piglet: 3, small, blue and white striped shirt, blue shorts, blonde hair, playful, happy, inquisitive, imaginative, spins around on heels, jumps up on people, cuddly, sweet, gentle
WOUNDED CHILD	George: mid-size, 14-16, baggy clothes, worn out, dull and drawn, sad, lonely, isolated, inward-looking and insular, looking down, curved shoulders, fight or flight, watching and observing, angry, hurt
LISTENER	Aaron: seated, gentle, open, caring, holding gaze, calm, contemplative, learned, bookish, glasses
DOER	Jack: overalls, hard at it, moving, energy, goal-setting, busy, relentless, hard-nosed, encouraging
ADVENTURER	Luke: shorts and t-shirt, excited, inquisitive, curious, friendly, open, relaxed, present, spontaneous, grateful, relaxed, foodie
THINKER	Saul: casual, inquisitive, questioning, time-rich, suggestive, bold
FEAR MONGER	Bryan: pajamas, unkempt, reclusive, negative, glass half empty, dark, restless, awkward, looking over shoulder, closed off, tired and grey
NAYSAYER	Marie: categoric, hardline, inflexible, always right, no reason, bemoaning, fearful

TASKMASTER	Joe: can-do attitude, everything is possible, impatient, now, guilt, hardworking, always on, striving, writhing, unsatisfied, loud, relentless, lack of joy, factual
DREAMER	Henri: light, playful, blue eyes, dark skin, warm, glowing, possibility, carefree, open-minded, accepting, ideas man, noncommittal, maybe

As you can see from Robert's list, each part has a role, a name, and a description, as if detailing a character in a play. These were the players in the inner landscape of his life, and the way they interacted with each other was determining his self-concept and his ideas of what he could accomplish.

In our work together, Robert's Dreamer was starting to come alive as he began to listen to his heart and trust his intuition more, growing his desire to pursue a new career. However, his Taskmaster was responding sternly to the Dreamer's novel ideas. During our sessions, we met with these parts in a guided visualization to help Robert release the emotional baggage he was carrying. This heaviness was constituted by harsh limitations of what the Taskmaster considered reasonable. Robert's burdens showed up in the visualizations as dense bags that he hefted onto his shoulders and could not seem to put down. It was as if he was quite attached to bearing this load, even though it was wearing him down. Who he would be without this weight was far scarier than the comfort of strict but familiar expectations.

In contrast to the heaviness of these bags, Robert's Dreamer part was hanging out paragliding in the sky! The Dreamer was weightless and airy, maybe excessively so. While the Dreamer loved paragliding, we discovered in time that he tended to hang out high above the ground to dwell in a detached fantasy realm where he could be safe from the influence of the unforgiving Taskmaster. The Taskmaster, when given a chance, would attack with a barrage of harsh words and unrelenting warnings of everything that could go amiss if Robert dared to stray from his current path (on which he was not very happy).

As we did more guided journeys, we helped the Taskmaster grow into a new role that would balance and even align with the Dreamer's aspirations. Soon, the Taskmaster realized that his approach was not even meeting his own needs, and he lightened his forceful demands, starting to become more supportive. As the Taskmaster opened to collaborating with the Dreamer, the Dreamer felt comfortable enough to come down from his parachute in the sky so that they could work as a team.

For Robert, taking the initial step to list these parts helped him gain perspective of the aspects at play within his mind and heart. The Parts Chart was the launchpad to help transform patterns that were hindering him. Several months later, Robert was happy to report that he applied for and got accepted into a master's program in a course of study which he initially felt was "too-good-to-be-true" but eventually permitted himself to pursue!

SOPHIA'S LIST OF PARTS AND THEIR IMPACT ON HER

Sophia was experiencing stress and anxiety around money and feeling inner pressure to "get her act together." She felt so much inner conflict about her next steps with her business that she even considered closing down shop if she could not find a way to make it work. We started with getting to know some of the parts in her inner landscape to see which might be contributing to her feelings of being stuck both personally and professionally. Sophia said her list took ten minutes to write out, and she was surprised at how easy it was to find these parts within herself.

SOPHIA'S PARTS	DESCRIPTION
SLOUCH COUCH GROUCH	Especially when I think I need to exercise, cook something healthy, or go out with friends or on a date, my Slouch Couch Grouch wants to be lazy and lounge on my sofa instead.
WIMP	This part causes me to stay too long in relationships, homes, or work that I've outlived and not follow through on novel desires. It has the feeling of putting its hands up like, "What's the use?"
BRAVE	This part shows up when I'm always choosing the road less traveled and making high-risk, gut-wrenching decisions that most people won't do, but I will.
ANXIOUS	This part causes me digestive issues and to lose sleep. This part is most nervous about not getting anywhere personally or professionally due to feeling that I'm running out of time and money.
CRITIC	The one that wants me to SNAP OUT of the Slouch/ Wimpy /Anxious moods. It's good in the sense that it wants me to act, but it is harsh about it.
BLOCK	When I lose trust that things will work out, my whole system shuts down as well as my faith and feeling of love. When in Block mode, I end up sitting on the fence and feeling stuck.
INTENSE	This part drives the tons of passion I have in what I do. I'm all in when I go for things. At the same time, there could be lots of anger as expressed through screaming or increasing volume of voice. Intense part shows up whether I like it or not.
ZEN	This part helps me relax my nerves and digestive system. It comes when I get to swim, be on the beach, or read a book.

SUNNY	This part is full of positive thoughts, action, freedom, and clarity. It is closer to self-contentment.
DREAMY	This part is where I would like to be. It's what I imagine when I want to write a book, travel, or live in a warmer place. It contains any stream of desires I may have.
INTUITIVE	This part has vision but is far from where others normally stand, making it hard to have a sense of belonging. My ability to sense things in advance makes me different from others, so where do I fit in?
CURIOUS	This part has me always learning something new. It generates movement, pushing me to forge ahead and discover what's next.
DEEP	This is the part of me that likes conversations and thoughts about life, people, nations, and the importance of connection.
THOUGHTFUL	This is my part that cares about others and hates violence or conflict.
EQUALIZER	I like what's fair and inclusive. That has informed my career path and what I stand for.
SILENCE	When this part is present, there are moments of internal thought far away from noisy and busy spaces. It quiets the voices in my head. I need seclusion time for this part to show up.

Sophia wrote so fluidly in her first round of listing that she had to stop herself at some point. She later returned to the list and fleshed out an additional five or six more parts, realizing this list could keep growing!

As she debriefed this activity, Sophia noticed a lot of inner conflicts. She said, "This might explain why I'm having issues walking away from things or even going into things. It feels like there's too much effort to get a consensus from all these voices to get to step number two."

When reflecting on her list, Sophia noticed that there was a balancing act between the "negative parts" and the "positive ones" that were keeping each other in check. Sophia felt that the back and forth between these groups created a stalemate that kept her from moving in any direction at all. For example, she mentioned, "If Slouch takes over for a day, the next day I won't slouch at all, but I'm still on the fence about what to do. I can't seem to make a decision [to keep my business going or to shut it down] because neither option seems attractive. So, I get into this stagnant mode because whatever I do doesn't seem to help push me forward to make any concrete choices."

Sophia realized that her inner system was not working well enough to serve her overall goals. Rather than being a well-oiled machine with all her parts collaborating in tandem, she felt pulled in many different directions. "There are too many cooks in the kitchen. There is a lot I like to do and want to explore, so I am getting lost in the curiosity of it all and not taking a specific stance."

When I asked Sophia what her relationship was to the parts on this list, she replied that overall she felt accepting of all her parts. She also admitted that she was not convinced that she was managing them all properly since, at the end of the day, she did not feel she was getting to where she wanted to be.

When we explored which parts were most currently active for Sophia, she said, "Lately, the Slouch, the Wimp, the Anxious, and the Block seem to be taking a lot of space. I am tired because they take up a lot of room. I want the sustainability and stamina that I had before."

Seeing this list gave Sophia a simple but straightforward resolve: "Today, I'm going to go to an exercise class to create movement and to separate myself from my indecision about my future path. That way, I hope my choices will come from a more inspired place rather than from my tendency to inspect or dissect everything. Since I am so intellectually oriented, going deeper into thought used to work, but not anymore!"

In starting to list out these parts and seeing how they interacted with each other, Sophia gained a fresh awareness, saying, "I did not realize there were parts that weren't even speaking with each other, so this is an eye-opener. This process gives me hope that there is work here that needs to be done and that there is a path to listen more to those parts and find cohesion to move ahead. The fact that I am aware these parts are here is new, and I can use this to move forward."

By the end of our time together, Sophia's work with parts had helped clear up the daily anxiety that had been constricting her into a state of paralysis. Her obsessive worry lifted, and she stopped fighting with herself. She grew more empowered to take responsibility for what was happening in her life rather than feeling like the victim of her circumstances and patterns.

By listing her parts, she could embrace all sides of herself and relax the fears that had controlled her. After a few months, she said, "I didn't know that I could give myself room to pause, but now that I have, I have less expectation of perfection and am more open to letting things go rather than obsessing over them." When she let go of the pressure that had constricted her imagination, she actually found new options to increase her revenue stream, opened herself up to dating again, and also completed her first book which had been on the back-burner for years!

As you can see from these examples, observing your parts in a list can lay the foundation for understanding what each part of you has to offer. By acknowledging how they live in you currently, you can begin to relate to them in a way that invites less tension and more peace.

MY FIRST PARTS LIST:
CLUSTERS OF CHARACTERS

When I first created my own list of 20 or so parts (in my 20s), I noticed themes emerging. It seemed that some parts were very connected to each other in terms of their personality and function, so I organized them into groups. Over a couple of years, I identified different parts that emerged in each category.

As an example, here are several of those categories:

PROTECTIVE/WOUNDED PARTS	CREATIVE/EXPRESSIVE PARTS
The Critic: negative self-talk, oppressive, limiting, scarcity mindset, skeptical, raised eyebrows	**The Muse:** creative, unbridled, boundless, imaginative and artistic, a painter and ribbon dancer
The Victim: conflicted, self-pitying, indulgent, dwells, self-doubting, unsure, regretful, resentful	**The Sparkler!:** exuberant, radiant and frenetic, fast-talking, excited and excitable
The Hustle Muscler: resourceful, strives, reaching, persistent, determined, survival-focused, resilient, drained, trying to prove something	**The Writer:** observant, thoughtful, in touch with depth, self-aware, reflective, eloquent, uncovers latent insights, brings truth to the surface

NATURE/MYTHICAL PARTS	LOVING/GIVING PARTS
The Flower Child: curious, open, trusting, pure of heart, easy-going, natural, loving, tender, kind, earthy, rolls down hills, innocent, lovable, eager	**The Lover:** serene, giving, blissful, gracious, connected, sweet, sensual, surrendered, companion, partner, romantic, committed
The Dolphin: go with the flow, joyful/joyous, silly, playful, deeply spiritual, communal, interconnected/interdependent, bright (intellectually, emotionally, spiritually)	**Higher Self/ Big Mind:** calm, knowing, restful, spacious, wise, deliberate/intentional, serene, placid, unfazed, steady/steadfast, reliable, accessible, and true
The Dreamer: wishful/wistful, eager, lives in possibility, thrives on imagined opportunities, optimistic, bright-eyed	**Guide/Facilitator:** [when coaching or leading groups especially] A teacher/mentor, holder of space, highly intuitive, nudges lovingly, reveals to others their own wisdom, tuned in, follows her higher callings

As you can see, the process of listing your unique parts is highly personal. It helps to see your representation of parts not as ones that you are creating out of nowhere but rather as aspects of your wholeness that you are unveiling to yourself. Your parts may take many forms as you get to know them, but their underlying essence is already there. By relating to both the forms and the essence, you receive insights about who you have been, who you are, and who you are becoming.

Be open-minded in uncovering your parts, listening for their names and receiving any imagery with your intuition rather than forcing personas out of what feels convenient or what you think you "should" write.

It is also important to note that, in this work, I distinguish the "You" who is the composite of all your parts from the parts themselves. One way to think about this work is like a game of chess in which the chess pieces are your different parts with individual roles, functions, abilities, and motives. Then, there is the larger field of awareness that witnesses and holds all the players and their actions—your Wise One Within, the chessboard. Finally, "You" are the chess player who can see the board and the pieces and ultimately relate to all of them and move accordingly.

If you are not able to sense specific names for your parts, it could be that they are so blended in your day-to-day experience that you have a hard time distinguishing them from "You." As an example, this could happen when your Inner Critic has been behind the steering wheel for so long that you think that way of looking at the world is just the way you are. In other cases, when some of your parts have a healthier role in your life, they might already be integrated and therefore not show up so distinctly. It could also be that a part is not currently active, so they could be harder to grasp or identify than when they are louder and more visible. In the next activity, get started by pulling a thread from wherever you have some initial clarity. Trust that as you go through the process, more understanding and self-connection will be revealed.

Lastly, as you read through the examples of parts above and create a list of your own, you may notice that it is easy to relate to certain parts, while others may seem less developed or less favorable to you. These "shadow side" parts might be easier to locate, though perhaps harder to accept. With some of these, it may be that another part of you views them as less attractive, and, therefore, you may feel more resistant to connecting with them. Trust that as you go along this journey, your relationship to your parts—and their relationships to each other—will evolve to include greater compassion.

In this chapter's activity, you will begin by crafting your list of parts and taking stock of your initial reactions to them so you have a sense of how you are already relating to them. Throughout the course of this book, you will learn to connect with these parts with curiosity, cultivating respect for each part's important role within your inner life.

CHAPTER 2 ACTIVITIES:

Making a Parts Chart

Reading this book without completing the activities is like trying to figure out what a peach tastes like just by its look and feel. To truly experience it, you must bite in. Engage with this book, and you will get the most out of it. The concepts will come alive for you. If you find you are reading and not doing the suggested prompts, take the opportunity to explore what part of you is resisting doing them and why.

Remember: Awareness of your parts is half the process! We will continue with another activity to take a big bite of that figurative peach.

MAKING YOUR
PARTS LIST

I first learned that, on average, we can typically name 9-20 parts off the top of our heads (Internal Family Systems posits that even the parts have their own parts!). For now, as the mind is a busy enough place as it is, we'll stick to the 9-20 as a starting point.

To begin working with parts, we must first know "who is in the room." Who are the current players in your mind and heart? That is what we will explore in this activity. We will create a list that you can add to and update as you go along. It may feel exciting, and it may feel daunting. Remember—this is the first glance, and you can always return to your list as it evolves.

Ready to try? Let's begin.

1) IDENTIFY AND DESCRIBE THEM *(20 minutes)*

Envision your different sides, aspects, modes, and roles.

Reminders:

› Everyone connects with parts in different ways that are unique to that person. Some people have feelings, colors, or shapes that emerge instead of personified characters. For others, every character is a slightly different version of themselves rather than a unique figure. Honor whatever arises, taking it seriously enough to take it lightly. In caring about this work, permit yourself to allow your process to flow rather than cling too tightly to preconceived ideas.

› I found it helpful to avoid imposing my thoughts about who should show up. It is important not to get too caught up in a fixed notion of the parts. Keep in mind that they can morph as you get to know them, as they continue to reveal themselves, and as they interact with each other. An open-minded awareness of your parts nourishes them in a way that makes space for their true nature to emerge.

Now, write down your parts in the order that you think of them, following the steps below:

a) Identify your parts by jotting down their names/titles as they come to mind.

Example: "Scrolly Trolly" who pops up when I feel insecure after too much time on social media.

b) Alongside the names, write down any characteristics and features (e.g. personality traits, age, height, shape, appearance, style of dress, demeanor, gender [if applicable], etc.).

Example: Scrolly Trolly is jealous, competitive, and resentful, a part of my "yuck brain" that takes over when scrolling through my newsfeed of

3,000 people. Still in his flannel navy blue pajamas, he has beady eyes that squint and roll sarcastically when viewing the latest post about a relative stranger's avocado toast, latest baby photo, or political opinion. Scrolly Trolly always has a snide and snarky remark he could post but usually keeps his mouth shut.

c) Some of the parts may have overlapping or similar qualities (ones in certain clusters can seem to be like cousins or even twins!). Intuitively assess which characters in the list may all be aspects of **one** part versus which roles seem to constitute separate entities with their own names and qualities.

Example: "Scrolly Trolly" might be a relative of "Impressive Irene," who wants to present only her highlight reel of curated photos online, or "Distractible Dave," who has opened up his social media sites for the fifteenth time within the hour to check them out of habit.

d) If you see a relation between subparts of a larger group, feel free to categorize under a heading such as: "Protective Parts" or "Creative Parts," etc. These might be clustered together with their own name.

Example: "My Image-Conscious Crew."

2) TAKE INVENTORY OF YOUR INITIAL RESPONSE TO YOUR PARTS *(15 minutes)*

Focus on four or five of the parts in your Parts Chart that elicited some immediate reaction, whether another part of you felt repelled, appreciative, or curious about them. Write an extra few words or lines about what arose for you in relation to those parts.

For example, which parts do you identify with most strongly or admire? Which are you rejecting? In Robert's case, he noticed that he wanted to fire parts that seemed to cause him trouble, whereas he felt a kinship with others. What is your current attitude toward each of your parts?

Since it is very likely that your reactions are actually other parts popping up with opinions in response to each other, you might ask: which (other) part of me is having that response?

Try not to get caught up in who you prefer. This is not a parts popularity contest. Notice your current responses to each part without judging the part.

Though you may recoil from some, do not shun parts you initially dislike or parts that seem useless. Trust that every part has a purpose and needs your loving attention to reveal their true nature.

3) CHAPTER 1 ACTIVITY REVISITED *(5 minutes)*

Return to your journal activity from Chapter 1.

a) You now know your parts much better and can see which could be at play at any given moment. Review what you wrote in your journaling in Chapter 1 about your visions and inner blocks.

b) Which parts are activated in relation to your dreams, championing your goals with enthusiasm and desire?

c) Which parts arise in relation to your inner barriers, potentially putting on the brakes?

See if you can match some of these parts you have now identified with the previous thoughts that simply felt like "You."

CHAPTER 2 KEY CONCEPTS

› Parts are aspects of yourself that you can relate to and seek to understand. They have their own interests, needs, desires, and emotions.

› When something triggers a part, they come into your awareness, giving you an opportunity to get to know them better.

› Making a list of parts that you already notice will help you to recognize what aspects comprise your mindscape and allow you to work with them.

› "You" are the composite of all the parts. You are influenced by their activity and can also influence them by relating to them.

› When parts are identified and noticed for what they are, they have less control of the reins that drive you to decisions that are out of alignment with your best path.

› In naming and listing your parts, you are creating some distance with which to see them and relate to them as aspects of yourself. This process helps you become more whole, rather than over-identifying with a single part.

› There are some common archetypal parts that you can use as a starting point, but your parts list will be as unique as you are.

› You will not need to memorize your parts list or view any part as static or fixed. This process is emergent, evolving with time.

› The goal of this chapter's activity is to list your parts as they appear today, taking stock of any feelings that arise toward each. In doing so, you will begin to flesh out your inner cast of characters, getting a sense of the key players in your psyche.

CHAPTER 3
BRINGING YOUR
PARTS TO LIFE

Visualize Your Parts to Cultivate

Relationships with Them

Art is the lie that enables us to realize the truth.

— PABLO PICASSO

The next component in becoming aware of our parts is to animate them through illustrating them. As the Picasso quote implies, capturing experiences through art might seem to render them narrow or static and thus deceiving. Yet, an art form can inspire us and reveal truth through our interpretations of it and what those reflect about us.

As we create or appreciate art, it becomes a mirror that shows us ourselves. If, for example, you draw your Inner Child, the depiction is merely a representation of this internal figure. Yet, the details you come up with will tell a story that illuminates the essence of this figure through how you depict and understand its form.

In this way, symbolizing our parts through representing them artistically allows us to forge deeper relationships with them and thus, with ourselves. In bringing our inner workings to life, we can navigate our feelings and circumstances with greater ease. We gain new emotional skills by meeting what is unfolding within us in a new way.

When we connect with the current truths that are expressed through our portrayals of our parts, these become stepping stones for future truths. We might even want to draw the same parts a few times to see how they evolve.

In Chapter 2, you took the first steps by meeting your parts, identifying them, and distinguishing them from each other. Now, by connecting with them visually, you will see their personalities take shape. Section I of this chapter will guide you to illustrate individual parts to understand each better. Section II will explain how to create a map depicting parts in relation to *each other,* thus shedding light on how they currently interact. Through these activities, you will more readily relate with each aspect of yourself and also uncover important relationships between your parts.

SECTION I:
ILLUSTRATING PARTS INDIVIDUALLY

To augment the verbal description of your parts list, let's add another layer by creating visual depictions. By doing so, you will bring to life many details, including the style and color of the parts' clothing, facial expressions, and postures. Illustrating the contours of your inner characters will help you relate to your parts energetically as well as cognitively. As you observe each part's unique characteristics in your drawings, you will also cultivate more intimacy with that aspect of yourself since you will notice traits about them you may not have otherwise seen.

Externally representing your parts as drawings will also allow you to relate to each one distinctly. Sometimes, you might identify with one aspect of yourself so strongly that you consider it the totality of your being. You may get caught up in a certain feeling and start to resign yourself to the idea that "this is just the way I am." By illustrating your parts, you can see each as one aspect of you among many. You will be able to hold what arises more lightly as just one piece of a larger equation.

MEETING MY PARTS ON PAPER

Sometimes, a teacher or mentor in our lives can say something that stays with us years later and continues to be applied in new ways. For me, this occurred in high school when we were exploring creative writing. When my English teacher instructed each of us to sketch the Inner Critic and the Inner Muse on separate sheets of paper, he introduced me to the power of illustrating parts of our inner lives, thereby animating their being.

As I drew these figures on the page, I witnessed how their imagery revealed a tension within me between wanting to fit in and wanting to stay aligned with my values. As a service-oriented teenager who mainly read books for fun, winning "cool points" with my peers was not my strong suit. In my junior year, I was spearheading a charitable initiative that I cared deeply about, a cause which I prioritized above popularity. My Inner Muse cared most about self-expression through writing as well as making a difference any way she could. On the other hand, my Inner Critic felt that if I did not make efforts to care about how others perceived me, I would continue to feel like an outsider at school.

I remember the drawings of both those parts as vividly as if I had them next to me today. The Inner Critic's portrait featured a thin, tall, attractive, young woman with stick-straight hair, whereas my own is naturally curly. She was wearing tight blue jeans paired with something I did not even own: a white fitted t-shirt from Abercrombie and Fitch—the fashionable brand at the time. I added word bubbles coming out of her stern, tight-lipped mouth, sentences that began with, *"You should . . . "* and *"You shouldn't . . . "* Looking at what I had drawn felt constricting and made me cringe.

My second picture portraying my Inner Muse provided a stark contrast to the conformist and judgmental Inner Critic. My Inner Muse was curvier, including her hair, which extended from her head in all directions like long black wild ribbons. She was wearing a rippling flowery top and an enormous orange and pink skirt with swirls on it, mirroring the curls from her head. She had a big smile and bore an expansive gesture with her arms flung into the air. Rather than being surrounded by word bubbles, I depicted her roaming freely on green grass, smiling from ear to ear. She was leaping about from the top of the hilly horizon line—and almost off the page! To my delight, my Inner Muse exuded a welcoming, self-assured, and fun energy.

Depicting these two characters visually helped me to connect with their vibe, observe what they cared about, and notice how they moved in my world. As I placed their portraits side-by-side, the Inner Critic's stiffness obviously contrasted the Inner Muse's carefree whimsy. The images before me felt like accurate representations of the push and pull between my unbridled, generous, creative self and my polite, socialized, and self-conscious side.

Encountering these two figures was a foundational experience for my deeper exploration of parts ten years later. Reflecting back now, I see that my Inner Critic longed for acceptance and belonging, whereas my Inner Muse longed for the freedom to be expressive, giving, and joyful. The Inner Critic thought I had to constrain myself to gain approval, whereas the Inner Muse was off in her own world and not considering social dynamics.

Since I felt so caged by the Inner Critic's admonishments, I idealized my Inner Muse and longed to embody more of her qualities. However, the integration needed would illuminate the value in both parts: the care the Inner Critic had for maintaining social dynamics that served my relationships and the authenticity my Inner Muse wanted to share by being emotionally vulnerable. Bringing these two parts together over the years would be vital in creating space for them to co-exist, come into balance, meet their needs, and share their gifts.

Coming up next in Chapter 4, we will explore how letting two sides of yourself speak to each other can illuminate latent dynamics and help you navigate places where you may feel polarized. Creatively bringing your parts to life visually serves as a helpful foundation for crafting a subsequent dialogue between these figures. Illustrating your parts gives you a window into what they care about and how they express themselves. When you compare your drawings side-by-side, you will be able to see what they share in common and what elements they have in contrast.

USING OTHER ARTISTIC MEDIUMS

Some might feel intimidated by sketching out their parts, fearing they lack talent as a visual artist. Skill with charcoal or colored pencils is not necessary to get an initial feel for your parts. Still, different mediums can bring out different perspectives. One alternative to drawing your parts is to make small collages of them using images from magazines. An effective way of doing this is inspired by SoulCollage®, an in-depth methodology of self-exploration created by Seena B. Frost.

I first encountered this modality at an Expressive Arts Therapy Conference in New York City. Having just moved, I was stressed from navigating all the new aspects of big city living. I looked forward to exploring my emotions through the collage workshop. Thematically assembling pictures from magazines onto large blank cards enabled me to express the impact this transition had on my inner world.

As we collected imagery, I immediately gravitated to a photo featuring two children dressed in white, laughing delightfully as they reveled in a pillow fight. I immediately added it to one of my cards to symbolize spontaneity, play, and getting lost in the moment. I surrounded it with playful purple spirals that I fashioned from a different magazine. Looking at the light-hearted part of me that emerged onto this card inspired a feeling of relief.

Later that week, I was rushing around, swept away in the bustle of the fast-paced city streets. Funnily enough, I happened to pass a mattress store, and the sign outside caught my eye. It was a standing poster with an advertisement—the exact image of those two gleeful children in mid-air jumping on the bed!

This meaningful coincidence made me perk up and remember my intention to cultivate more levity and presence in my day. Since imagery is powerful, having a picture in your mind can create a symbolic doorway to a universal idea that takes on personal meaning.

You may have other visual art forms you enjoy, such as working with clay to make figurines or using paints to create a scene for each part. Feel free to use the modality that inspires you the most.

—

Now, you will try your hand at drawing several of your parts. You can use the examples and instructions in the activity to follow as a jumping-off point. After that, in the second section of this chapter, you will create a map that elucidates the relationships between your parts.

CHAPTER 3 ACTIVITY FOR SECTION I:

Draw Your Parts Individually

To begin, look at your parts list and select two parts that create some dissonance when you think of them. Then, choose two more that stimulate curiosity or appreciation.

You may have come across two parts in conflict from your journaling in Chapter 1 or your list in Chapter 2. If so, of the four you choose today, select at least one pair that seem to hold differing perspectives from each other.

Then, choose one of the three artistic mediums below to bring them to life.

I. DRAWING OR PAINTING *(1 hour)*

› Draw each of the four parts you chose to connect with more deeply. Your illustration could be a sketch with a pencil, colored markers, watercolor, or even a digital tool.

› Ideally, each should be on their own piece of paper and can be depicted standing alone in a posture that suits them or in an environment that is comfortable for them.

› We are not going for Monet here. There is no perfect way to do this. Just sketch your parts out as best you can—even stick figures count!

› You can use word bubbles or thought bubbles where appropriate to include key phrases or words that tend to emanate from a particular part.

› Make sure you have ample time blocked out so you can do this in a relaxed way. You can play soft, inspiring background music if you find that this supports the creative atmosphere.

Reminder: The purpose of this process is not to set your parts in stone but rather to help you symbolize your parts through drawings so you can interact with them meaningfully.

Below are examples from my cast of inner characters. I used a digital application to illustrate these key players who frequently arose in relation to each other.

MS. PRESENCE

MS. SUCCESS

CORE SELF

VICTIM VICTORIA

ABUNDANTIA

STRESSED OUT SALLY

MERRY MUSE

2. DIGITALLY *(1-2 hours)*

›   Instead of drawing your parts, you could use a search engine online to find images that symbolize each of these parts' tone and style. In this way, you could locate an image or assemble a collection of images that you feel correspond to each of the four parts you chose to work with today.

›   When I first created a Pinterest board for my Ms. Success part, I found that I was collecting images of some societally informed markers of success. Though some of them seemed foreign or exaggerated to me, they were symbols I thought would appeal to her. These included photos of shiny red high heels, stacks of money, a shiny engagement ring, a fancy fountain pen, and models dressed in powerful pantsuits. In contrast, my Dreamer part's board included flowing water fountains, trellises, body glitter, crowns of flowers, and gardens with hanging outdoor lanterns.

›   It is okay if your part seems like a bit of a caricature at first. Their nuance and subtleties will show up more as you get to know them better. Try not to overthink the process, but rather observe with curiosity what reveals itself through this exploration.

3. SCRAPBOOKING *(2-3 hours)*

›   If you would like to work with collage, first gather a pile of unrelated magazines with a variety of images. To keep the parts you chose top of mind, you may want to write each of their names down on a separate piece of paper and spread these out on your workspace.

›   Begin by cutting out images that spark an emotion. Photos that either attract you or repel you are great fodder to begin. You do not have to immediately know which picture will go where. However, if you do get a sense of where an image belongs, then you can place that image in the corresponding pile for that part.

› When you finish collecting images that you feel are poignant, start to assemble them into a collage for each part. You can represent a part with an amalgamation of images—including objects, plants, and animals that illustrate the archetype or energy of that part. It can be nice to have a background image as the scenery and then layer smaller, more specific cutouts on top of it.

› When assembling your collage, you may not initially know why a particular image is calling you. Yet, as you let your exploration lead you in assembling it, a meaning can reveal itself upon reflection. The process can be similar to journaling, where you begin by putting your pen to a blank page, following the thread of an idea. Eventually, the exploration leads you to a fully formed conclusion that may not have been obvious when you started. As always, follow your instincts with what you create, even if some of what emerges is unexpected. You can explore its significance to you afterward.

› An excellent method for working with images is the practice of SoulCollage® in which you can assemble depictions of your inner archetypes through an intuitive process, creating a card for each part of yourself as a method of self-discovery. For more information on that particular method, please check out founder Seena B. Frost's work and website, listed in the "Resources" section at the back of this book.

Suggestions:

› As you draw, paint, or collage your parts, you may want to create a binder or a scrapbook where you can keep them all together. When you complete more activities in this book, you can add them to the collection.

> When you revisit this activity in the future to depict additional parts, you may want to experiment with a different style or modality than the one you chose today.

> Since parts are evolving, feel free to draw the same parts again at a later date and observe any differences.

SECTION II:
VISUALIZING THE WEB OF
CONNECTIONS BY MAPPING PARTS

Mind mapping is a great tool to see the relationships between parts. The basic idea of a mind map is to visually plot anything you are holding in your mind so you can take inventory of what is at play in your current thought process.

One way to make a mind map is to connect all your ideas, options, or opportunities in different places on the page. In this way, mind mapping is often used in decision-making because it allows you to see all your options and considerations in one place. Making a similar map in the context of parts allows you to organize your various inner players spatially and relationally so you can take stock of your inner world.

In our next activity, you will create a parts map of the whole cast that you have encountered so far. Creating a visual web of connections will help you get a sense of how different parts are related to each other. For example, you will be able to see which parts are working in harmony or at odds. This map will illuminate which parts may be central to you, looming large, or not getting enough attention.

You can create your parts map with markers, post-it notes, or even online with certain digital tools. You will begin by charting all your parts inside of bubbles, perhaps making each bubble's size correspond with how much each takes up space in your current inner system. You can place the different parts near or far from each other depending on which you determine might be in a group or cluster and which are quite foreign to each other or even antagonized.

As you plot your parts, you can draw lines between them that signify their relationships. For example, you could draw a red-dotted line of x's to depict a dissonant relationship between two parts versus a solid green line to show a collaborative connection. You can use whatever combination of colors and shapes you want, making a key to indicate what each type of line means.

Here is an example of what a parts map could look like:

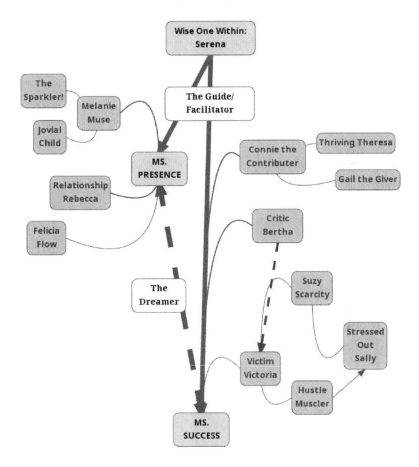

I used a digital format via MindMup to create this sample map (see previous page) of the clustered parts listed in my parts charts in Chapter 2 **https://www.mindmup.com/**

After you have plotted all the parts, you can rank specific criteria on a scale from 1-10 to take the pulse on various elements at play. You could assess how much you currently identify with that part, how much you believe you like/dislike it, or how active it is for you. For example, if you choose to rank how familiar each part is to you, a low score (1-3) might mean it feels foreign or surprising, and a high score (7-10) might mean you are very aware of this part's presence and ways of being. Ranking different elements related to each part will help you get a more detailed picture of how you (or other parts) are currently relating to its presence. Feel free to make the activity your own and organize it in a way that makes sense to you as you go through the process.

As with the parts list, the map that you create today will be merely a snapshot that gives you insight into the current dynamics within you that can continually evolve. In fact, the awareness you gain from simply creating the map may itself shift your relationship to these parts and their relationships to each other. If you redo this exercise a few weeks from now, it may look completely different. As you continue to connect with your parts, you will come to appreciate that they are dynamic forces within you as well as important catalysts for growth!

In the following examples of parts mapping, each person adapted the activity according to interpretations and insights that arose from their explorations.

AYLA'S MAP DISCOVERING
HOW PARTS HELP OR HINDER
EACH OTHER

Ayla used a hand-drawn map to reveal the dynamics between her parts as well as her own relationship to each part. Through this process, she realized which parts she appreciated and wanted to bolster and which ones she felt were holding her back and thus needed more loving attention.

Ayla felt she had spent much of her life going through the motions and living by other people's rules. Growing up surrounded by much anxiety in her household, Ayla developed a fear of uncertainty that dictated her choices. Feeling she had to play by the rules, she picked a "safe" major and career path in college. This conforming tendency informed a part she called Practical/Norms/Safe Options.

Once Ayla decided to engage in life coaching and therapy, she started connecting with her true values. She began considering how to live life more on her own terms. That is when a new part arose in her awareness: The Questioner of Social Norms. This part came into play as Ayla started feeling that she could live more purposefully. Ayla explained, "This part adds a lot of fulfillment and confidence to my life because I feel happy knowing I am making decisions for myself." Fostering this part even helped her make the leap to leave New York City and start a brand-new life in a countryside town in New Hampshire!

In her parts mapping process, Ayla ranked her initial responses to her parts. She made a key in the left-hand bottom corner of her map indicating what criteria she was assessing (dislike, enjoy & appreciate, how active, and how familiar). As she reflected on these metrics, Ayla was surprised to find that most of these parts were more familiar to her than she had realized since she had numbered them all 7 or above in that category. She also saw that Anxiety and Inner Critic/Insecure were both parts that she currently disliked at a level 10 out of 10 and only appreciated at a level 2 out of 10. Those parts were also strongly connected, as indicated by a thick black line.

Ayla felt that the Anxiety and Inner Critic/Insecure duo stimulated an aversion to any risk outside of the status quo. They were bound together in an unhelpful alliance that appeared to have such a negative effect on Ayla's life that she tensed up just thinking of them. When we see parts like this that stimulate such internal reactions in us, it is a good signal that they need more love and attention. Approaching even our disliked parts with compassion is a topic we will explore more in Chapter 5.

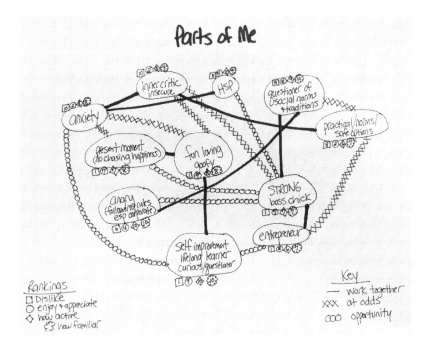

Though at first she was unsure if she would be able to identify her parts, making this map sparked many ideas for Ayla. She soon identified parts such as: HSP (Highly Sensitive Person), Practical/Norms/Safe Options, and Present Moment (no chasing happiness). She created cords between them to signify how these parts related to each other presently. She chose to

represent the opportunities for parts to collaborate by drawing a chain link between them.

Ayla also found that some pairs worked together in surprising ways. For example, her Inner Critic/Insecure and Strong Boss Chick had a dynamic that was activated whenever Ayla felt unsettled about not being taken seriously. If she felt disrespected in her day job, Ayla would feel anger and defiance arise, activating the Strong Boss Chick. This part held the desire to become self-employed and collaborated positively with Entrepreneur, as indicated by a dark solid line. Strong Boss Chick's commitment to maintaining self-respect fueled Ayla's desire to branch off on her own, even inspiring Ayla to begin building a business on the side.

As a result of making this map, Ayla intentionally began connecting with specific parts that she wanted to strengthen. For example, she gave Fun Loving Goofy a level 9 out of 10 for "enjoy and appreciate" and even placed it on her map first. Still, Ayla felt she had been estranged from this part for a long time. This joyful part had been antagonized by parts like Anxiety and Inner Critic/Insecure, as depicted by the "xxxxx" lines between those parts and Fun Loving Goofy. Ayla's worry about what others thought of her—coupled with feeling confined by her corporate job—suppressed this goofy part over time. Now, Ayla wanted this part to be more active. To reestablish a connection with this part, she planned to take an improv class that would engage Fun Loving Goofy in an environment that would help it come alive.

Making this map was a first step for Ayla in thinking about her parts both as individuals and as an interrelated inner community. Through reflecting on this map, she saw more clearly how the interactions of her parts in her internal world created decisions, opportunities, and challenges in her outer experience. From there, she was able to connect more with what was most important to her and take the steps toward freedom and independence both in her career and personal life.

MILANA'S MAP DISCOVERING
TWO SIDES OF THE SAME COIN

Milana shifted her perspective on her parts over time, creating both an original and an updated version of her hand-drawn parts map. A few months after completing her first version, she illustrated the map anew according to her inner changes. Seeing the progression of her inner relationships laid out on paper gave her interesting insights.

Milana, a mom and accountant, was exploring her spiritual side through pursuing a yoga teacher certification. She had only begun to explore her inner parts and was looking forward to getting to know herself through this lens. Initially, she organized her parts into "positive, high vibration parts" in the top right corner of the page, and "negative, low vibration parts" on the bottom left.

In the center of the map, Milana wrote out qualities that she felt were neither positive nor negative, but essential characteristics belonging to her Wise One Within, named Freedom. Milana described those traits, including Sensitive, Deep Thinker, and Intuitive, as key pieces of her personality that felt inseparable from who she was as a person.

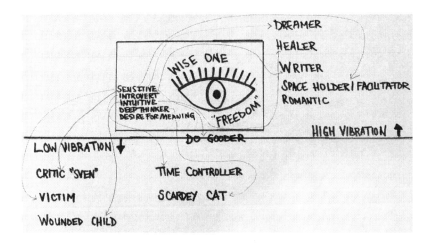

Milana's Map 1 (see previous page): As Milana first learned about parts, she clustered all of them into either "high vibration" or "low vibration" categories. In drawing this map, she noticed that the parts in both seemingly opposed categories corresponded to a core quality of her Wise One (centrally featured). Thus, these "high" and "low" vibration parts literally met in the middle.

From drawing this map and organizing these parts, Milana found a very interesting insight: all the "high vibration" and "low vibration" aspects were actually different expressions of the same core quality! Milana drew thin lines linking those "high vibration" or "low vibration" parts to their corresponding core traits in the center section. This illustrated how these seemingly opposed groups of parts were in some way connected to each other, literally meeting in the middle.

For example, Milana's Wounded Child (low vibration) was linked to her core trait of being Intuitive. However, that same Intuitive state was also connected to her Healer (high vibration). This realization speaks beautifully to Carl Jung's idea of the Wounded Healer—the concept that the places of our own hurt sometimes become the gifts we have to offer others.

Milana's first map is a vivid illustration of how every light casts a shadow and how every shadow indicates a light. Our inner aspects can showcase our strengths and pose challenges at the same time. For example, our sensitivity can have the bright side of helping us be more perceptive and empathic with others. Yet, it might also have a shadow side, such as when we take things too personally and feel insecure around others. Milana depicted her Sensitive part as a dreamer and a romantic who wanted to do good in the world. Yet, at the same time, she shared that this part could also get controlling and critical and make her feel like a victim. Milana felt torn between the push and pull of these apparently "high" and "low" places within herself that seemed to counteract each other in her life, keeping her stuck.

At first, Milana felt a bit judgmental toward her "low vibration" parts, wanting to overcome the ways she felt they held her back. I encouraged her to consider how on a deeper level they all shared an essence with the other parts, which she deemed to be more elevated. For example, her Time Controller felt like a "bad" part. However, we discovered that underneath its stressful and micro-managerial concerns about time, this part had a strong desire to make a difference. Its controlling behavior stemmed from its fear of wasting a single moment, precisely because this part was connected to how each breath is a gift! The Time-Controller's value was that it helped Milana to prioritize her responsibilities and set her up for success. Milana stated, "While reflecting on this map more deeply, I see the opportunity to see my parts in a different light. I can now notice how the parts I categorized as having a 'low vibration' actually have strengths that can serve me on my path."

After analyzing her map, Milana decided that she wanted to appreciate all the parts' value. Making a parts map can shine a light on previously unseen elements within, thereby changing the very inner landscape that was being illustrated. As such, Milana read through the rest of this book and created a new map demonstrating her evolved relationship with her inner system.

Depicting these new insights in an updated map resulted in a new portrayal for Milana:

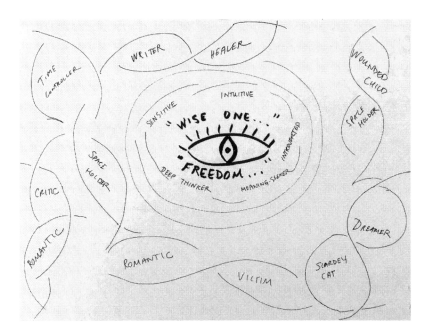

Milana's Map 2: This second more integrated map conveys a deeper under-standing of all the parts' roles. Here, each part is intertwined with the others, forming a braid around the Wise One Within. The initial hier-archical classification between "high" and "low" parts is replaced by a connectedness that shows how all parts are valuable in their interplay.

Milana shared her thoughts about her second map: "It has the same words in the middle but is presented in more of a flowing, connected, and circular format. The idea is that the inner circle is unraveling into braids. The parts (listed in the word bubbles) are each a piece of the braid. They are all coming together. I understand now that I can't have any of the parts without the inner circle qualities that unite them. Also, each of the parts enables the others to exist. They are all intertwined."

Milana explained that this second map felt much more integrated. When she reflected on its meaning, she realized it created a sense of calm and peace in her. She continued, "It was a big realization that the formerly low vibration and high vibration items actually are so connected. They feed each other. I was thinking of them very separately, but they all exist in relationship to each other without hierarchy."

Now, it is your turn to sketch out an initial map and see what it can reveal about your inner world!

CHAPTER 3 ACTIVITY FOR SECTION II:

Parts Mapping

BY HAND *(1 hour)*

1. GATHER YOUR MATERIALS

Gather colored pencils, markers, or the medium of your choice and a large piece of paper.

2. REVIEW YOUR PARTS LIST

Do the parts in your list have anything in common? See if you can identify clusters that appear related or a thread that unites any of them. Are some of them fast friends, while others seem opposed? Note any observations that come up when you review your list that might help you plot your parts.

3. PLOT YOUR PARTS

Choose the first part to add to the map. It could be the one that feels the loudest or the one you think is the most valuable or interesting.

You can check in with your intuition and eyeball the paper before making a mark. How does the left-hand corner feel to place this part? Or the bottom right? What about smack dab in the center of the page? You might sense that one area just feels more aligned than another.

Write that part's name in a circular bubble somewhere on the page where you intuit it belongs. The size of each bubble may represent how much space it currently takes up within you. Once you have mapped the first one, add all the others one by one in relation to each other in the same way.

Artistic option: If you prefer to create scenery for your map, feel free to illustrate the environment and draw little labeled figures for each part rather than using only bubbles.

4. ILLUSTRATE THE CONNECTIONS

After you plot the parts, look at the scene.

› Which parts on the map have an affinity? Would you characterize them as on a squad, distant cousins, or connected at the hip?

› Are any inner committees that tend to cluster together?

› Which parts are in opposition? Are they as far as they can possibly be from one another or at a calculated distance? Or, are they head-to-head and of equal stature?

Now, illustrate these relationships by connecting each part to other parts with different kinds of lines. You can indicate the nature of these connections with colors, shapes, or both.

For parts that seem to collaborate:
Find a way to symbolize that these parts are symbiotic and work together for your good, such as creating a line composed of a chain of small hearts or connecting them with a bold solid green line.

For parts that seem to be at odds:
Find a way to symbolize that these parts do not get along and are antagonized right now, such as drawing a line of xxxx's linking them together or sketching a thin line composed of red dashes (like minus signs).

If possible, make the connections obvious on your map so it is easy to interpret. To make it even clearer, you can make a key in the corner to explain the meaning of your lines. Then, see what happens as you literally connect the dots!

5. RATE WHAT MATTERS TO YOU *(Optional)*

Choose a few qualities, such as how much you think you like/dislike each part or how active it is in your life and rate the metric on a scale from 1-10. Write each number in a specific color as it corresponds to a certain meaning. You can generate your own criteria or use any of the guidelines below:

1-10 RED: How much you feel some aversion arise in relation to this part with 1 meaning, "It's fine, it doesn't seem to bother any other part of me" and 10 meaning, "Some part of me can't stand it and wish it would go away!"

1-10 BLUE: How much you enjoy and appreciate this part with 1 meaning, "I'm finding it hard to see this part as likable" and 10 meaning, "This part feels so easy for me to love and accept immediately!"

1-10 GREEN: How active this part is in you with 1 meaning, "Not very present, it feels a bit in the background" and 10 meaning, "It seems to run the show around here!"

1-10 ORANGE: How familiar you are with this part with 1 meaning, "It's completely new to me! I have a lot to learn" and 10 meaning, "It's my bestie/sidekick" or, "I can't get its voice out of my head!"

1-10 PURPLE: How identified are you with the part with 1 meaning: "I can't believe that's even a part of me!" and 10 meaning, "This is SO me, it's central to who I am!"

Use any metric that works for you based on what you would like to assess.

6. REFLECT ON YOUR PROCESS AND YOUR MAP:

How you do this activity can reveal parts of you and potentially even be a mirror for how you approach other areas of your life too, so take some time now to look back.

Reflection prompts:

› How was the process of making this map? Did it start out challenging and become easier? Were you striving for perfection or exploring playfully?

› For the parts that appear to be opposed, what do they have a hard time seeing eye to eye about?

› For those that are collaborating or aligned, what values do they share?

› For your metrics/rankings, what can you learn from reflecting on the numbers you listed? Do you notice any patterns?

› Journal about what you notice in this panorama of your current experience with your parts and what it might mean to you.

Note: You can add to this or remake the map as you get to know more parts and as your relationships with them—and their relationships to each other—evolve.

DIGITALLY *(1 hour)*

You can also use digital tools, such as MindMup or others, to create flowcharts online for free. Use the same process as above for your parts map, with the added ability to edit and shift bubbles around as needed.

Note: Though the maps featured in this book are depicted in black and white, you can use color with your map if you like. For example, you might fill each bubble with a color that corresponds meaningfully to each part, like red for a desirous or angry part or green for a growth-oriented or nature-loving part.

CHAPTER 3 KEY CONCEPTS

› Illustrating your parts offers a creative, playful, and imaginative space to connect with those parts most active in your inner system.

› You can draw your parts or make collages (with magazines or digitally) to help bring them and their characteristics to life so that you can gain insight from these representations.

› Drawing your parts is like putting a face to a name. With your freshly made illustrations or collages, you will have a more visceral connection to these aspects of you. In getting to know them better, you will have more ease relating to each part with more compassion.

› Parts mapping gives you an awareness of the dynamics and relationships present inside of you. In this interconnected web, you can plot each part in relation to the others to see how they are currently interacting. This activity gives you a sense of which parts are central, looming large, neglected, allied, or at odds.

› The representations of your individual parts, combined with your parts map, will provide visual cues for developing your dialogues between parts, which you will craft next in Chapter 4.

II.

WELCOMING
ALL OF YOU

So far, we have brought awareness to our inner lives by identifying and visualizing the parts at play within you. Section II is devoted to parts' relationships—both our relationship to our parts and their relationships with each other.

In these next chapters, you will explore the interactions between conflicting parts to identify their dynamics and connect with their underlying needs. You will learn to engage with your parts from a compassionate stance so you can allow them to shift from keeping you stuck to helping you feel more aligned. Lastly, you will apply this approach to your Inner Critic so it may evolve into being a force of contribution to your life.

CHAPTER 4
WHEN PARTS DISAGREE

Shift from Inner Conflict to Common Ground

*Your soul is oftentimes a battlefield, upon which your reason and your
judgment wage war against your passion and your appetite.
Would that I could be the peacemaker in your soul, that I might turn
the discord and the rivalry of your elements into oneness and melody.
But how shall I, unless you yourselves be also the peacemakers, nay,
the lovers of all your elements?*

*Your reason and your passion are the rudder and the sails of your
seafaring soul. If either your sails or your rudder be broken, you can but
toss and drift, or else be held at a standstill in mid-seas.
For reason, ruling alone, is a force confining; and passion, unattended,
is a flame that burns to its own destruction.*

*Therefore let your soul exalt your reason to the height of passion, that
it may sing; And let it direct your passion with reason, that your passion
may live through its own daily resurrection, and like the phoenix rise
above its own ashes.*

— KAHLIL GIBRAN, ON REASON AND PASSION, *THE PROPHET*

As the ever-eloquent Lebanese-American writer Kahlil Gibran describes in this timeless passage, we can feel ruled by two opposing forces, and we can lose ourselves if either one runs wild without the other. In this chapter, we will work with those polarized sides, which might represent your Reason and embody your Passion. Parts like these which have manifested in such extreme ways can often seem like enemies. When we dedicate time to get to know them and help them understand each other, we can integrate these parts more seamlessly. Doing so enables us to relate more lovingly toward these aspects of ourselves, bringing them into better balance with each other.

At the end of Chapter 1, you journaled about your vision and your blocks, examining what you want and what is in the way. In Chapters 2 and 3, you identified and illustrated some of the parts responsible for dreaming big or slamming the brakes in fear. In this chapter, you will get to explore the parts of you that are in apparent conflict and delve deeper into the causes of strife that keep them gridlocked in opposition. By crafting a dialogue between these two antagonistic parts, you will learn about what they truly need, potentially revealing common ground.

I have found dialoguing between parts to be especially useful when I am having a hard time deciding between two options that seem mutually exclusive. For example, some years ago, I found that I had a subconscious belief that I could either succeed in my career *or* in a romantic relationship, but not both. A part of me thought that devoting myself to a new relationship meant waving goodbye to my most cherished professional and creative goals. Another part acknowledged that focusing so intensely on those very goals might make it hard to care for any imaginary future children. Thus, in not wanting to choose one over the other, I unconsciously hesitated to pursue either of these paths fully!

In exploring this matter in the context of parts, I encountered Ms. Presence and Ms. Success. Ms. Presence represented the part of me that loved to meditate, do yoga, and nurture close relationships. She was in touch with the moment, thriving off a feeling of serenity and connection. Ms. Presence was family-oriented, wanting to find a long-term partner and settle down to enjoy the small everyday things in life. Ms. Success, on the other hand, was future-oriented and relentlessly driven to accomplish big things. She was ambitious, with an insatiable desire to contribute and achieve a legacy worthy of her potential. She was all business, brisk, and singularly focused on, well, success! As you can see in the drawings of each of these parts in Chapter 3, Ms. Success is very quantitatively driven, while Ms. Presence is all about the quality of her life experiences.

As I was on the threshold of starting my own business, I decided to bring to light this tension between Ms. Presence and Ms. Success by letting them talk to each other about my future. Through writing, then reading, their dialogue, I discovered the unconscious beliefs that had been driving me for years. In seeing these two sides of me come alive, I gained a clarity that helped me shift from unhelpful inner friction to inner collaboration.

COMMITTEE MEETING BETWEEN MS. SUCCESS AND MS. PRESENCE

Topic: Jeanine's Career Path

Ms. Success: I'm so glad you could leave your field of flowers long enough to show up for this meeting!

Ms. Presence: *That's* how you are going to greet me? Whatever happened to a good old-fashioned "Hello"? I'd even take a simple "Hi."

Success: *(tightly)* Alright, I'll take it easy on the sarcasm. Are you ready to dive in?

Presence: *(small sigh)* Yes, let's do this.

Success: Okay, we have to talk about what to do about our human's career path. She's at a poignant turning point right after graduating and needs direction to ensure her *success.*

Presence: Right, she's considering taking some temporary administrative jobs to pay the bills while thinking about following her passions and taking the plunge into entrepreneurship. So exciting!

Success: Terrifying and nauseating is more like it. Paying the bills doing something she doesn't even enjoy, and then setting off on her own—it sounds risky!

Presence: Well, there are always risks in living a life of love and passion—and what in the human realm do you remember being *certain?*

Success: Look, our girl has a lot going for her: She is creative, driven, and energetic, and she has got lots of potential. I want her to put it to good use and come out on top in the process.

Ms. Presence starts eating an apple, making a loud crunching noise.

Success: Hey! Are you going to take this seriously or not?

Presence: *(offering some apple apologetically)* Oh, sorry. Did you want some?

Success: No! Let's focus, please.

Presence: I am focusing. On what you're saying and on this apple. It is *delicious!*

Success: *(eye roll)* Okay, so—what are your great ideas about this situation?

Presence: Do you really care to know, or is this more sarcasm?

Success: Well, you know I'm not allowed to do this without you *(tries to soften)*. So, go ahead. Tell me what you think about all this.

Presence: I get that you are concerned for Jeanine because you believe that she must make many efforts in the realm of "doing." But your constant harping on "accomplishment" has created so much pressure in her life. She is so scared to experience any failure that she won't even try to—

Success: Hey! that's not—

Presence: —Not finished...! *(takes a breath)* So, while I understand you want what's best for her—or what you *think* is best for her—I would prefer you ease up on the gas pedal a bit because it's making her stressed and not helping your cause.

Success: You have a better idea, I suppose?

Presence: I don't want her to have regrets either, but I think she should be permitted to *enjoy* her life—the big things *and* the little things. I think she would thrive by savoring her relationships with her family and friends, and one day a family of her own! As she builds her future, I want her to soak in the small miracles of life too, like the way the dew glistens on the grass, the softness of a kitten, the colors of paint on her wall, the scent of lemon bread baking, the—

Success: Yes, yes, yes, we know! *(exasperated sigh)* You are so happy to get lost in the moment and all its glories. It sounds really nice, but you know she could end up failing pretty quickly if all she does is frolic around with her head in the clouds—like you!

Ms. Presence pauses, clearly taken aback and on the brink of tears. Ms. Success sees the words leave her mouth and regrets them, looking down sheepishly.

Presence: *(softly, slowly)* That wasn't nice . . .

Success: I know. I'm sorry . . . but the world isn't always nice either. She needs to be prepared. She needs to consider the important things.

Presence: And what are those?

Success: Well, to be supported in all her needs, starting with the basic ones. Food, shelter, and some long-term thinking would be nice. And then, of course, mental, emotional, and spiritual well-being. I fear that if she just "follows her dreams," she's going to be disappointed later if—or when—it does not work out in the magical way we might hope.

Presence: Okay, I hear you. I actually agree with you. Of course, I want her to be taken care of too and to be able to provide for herself in all those ways. But I also believe she can make that happen by offering the contribution that she came to make. My feeling is that she will find that in the *being,* not the doing. Because even if she has everything you could ever want for her, it is nothing at all if she can't *appreciate* it. I don't want her to lose the preciousness of these moments on earth by being so caught up trying to "make the most of them" that she then misses making the most of them!

Success: Okay, so you're saying that Jeanine's quality of life and *how* she does things is as important as what she does? Hmm . . . Well, I suppose that if she slowed down and was more present, she could gain more clarity in her next steps. I would like to see her centered enough to take smart, intentional, and well-calculated steps forward. I see that this would be better than blindly getting caught up in a pattern of racing around, chasing something that she will always find elusive.

Presence: Yes, I believe that if she approaches her tasks with love, grace, and *presence*, she will gain more fulfillment from these activities and will feel more peace inside of herself.

Success: Hmm, *fulfillment.* I like that! Especially feeling *full* from all her dreams becoming a reality!

Presence: Well, yes. Fulfillment bridges your emphasis on accomplishment and thriving and my focus on contentment within that achievement. Because it seems like you want the best for Jeanine, after all, too?

Success: Of course, I do. I think enjoying things is great too, but not when it means getting lost in a dream world. There's not *just* the present—the present is also composed of both the past and the future, so we need to take those into account as well.

Presence: That's true. You are just so often so hard on me and so demanding that I don't know what else to do except to retreat and find my own happy place. It really is so much effort and a struggle to keep up with your grand ambitions, and it robs me of the joy of just living my life now. Is there a way we can head towards these goals without suffocating the fun in the process?

Success: I think so. I do see how stillness and a softer approach can help us. However, I still argue that success is important too. To my mind, success is a second part or another stage of fulfillment. It occurs when you share your gifts with others and make a positive and valuable impact.

Presence: I can appreciate that satisfaction can come *both* from the meaningful relationships I hold dear *and* from taking inspired actions toward outcomes that you care about. I would like to help make Jeanine's doings into an expression of her being!

Success: Sounds good. So, can we agree to let her know to do her best, to work hard—but not too hard—and to let enough be enough?

Presence: *(smiling)* Yes. And then she can let enough be . . . everything.

These two parts initially appear quite polarized in this example, though they each carry wisdom. Ms. Success is a powerhouse of ambition regarding legacy, career, and contribution, sometimes at the expense of inner satisfaction and contentment. Ms. Presence wants more ease and enjoyment in the day-to-day, sometimes at the cost of visioning or preparing for the future.

Before doing this dialogue, I admired Ms. Success but felt oppressed by her stern, deadline-oriented approach. On the other hand, I felt relaxed by Ms. Presence, but felt she was a bit in la-la land and too lax. When putting them together, I got to see how their being at odds brought out the worst in each of them. This meeting helped to level the playing field, bring out new sides of them, and help them get on the same team. Working in tandem, they could join in making joyful progress toward long-term goals.

In writing this dialogue, I realized that these two were not bound to my original conception of them. Instead, their interactions with each other allowed them to harness their individual gifts while embracing what the other had to offer. In addition, it seemed the reason they were so extreme in the first place was that they were interacting in a reactive manner with each other rather than working together harmoniously.

In arguing with—or avoiding—each other, they further isolated the other and remained in conflict. They were pitted against one another, which caused an internal ping-ponging within me. However, through dialogue, these parts began to create a plan that would satisfy both of their needs. This new approach spoke to their shared *interests,* despite their apparently opposed positions. In dialoguing further, they could come to understand that Ms. Success's emphasis on contribution and Ms. Presence's focus on relationships and building a family were not mutually exclusive.

By consulting the parts at play, I learned how to address my inner conflict and access some truth underneath the layers of mental struggle. This insight offered me relief and renewed confidence in taking the next right step. After writing this dialogue, I became open to opportunities that I had been blocking without even knowing it. Later that year, I began a new relationship after years of being single and simultaneously enjoyed the most success that I had yet found in my career path.

It is important to note that while reconciliation may happen through interaction in dialogues like these, it cannot be forced. In other words, try to follow the flow of what each part is feeling and do not try to impose a tidy solution. It is not necessary to tie up loose ends in a bow for the sake of the exercise. Even just putting these parts together in a room can provide insight, which is a valuable step in transformation.

Let's look at another example of parts at odds with each other to see how each dialogue is unique.

MUSE AND CRITIC

Two related parts that often appear as a dueling duo are our old friends, the Muse and the Critic. As we mentioned in Chapter 3, the Muse archetype is often the seat of your dreams and exciting visions. On the other hand, the Critic often has some really good ideas from parents, guardians, and society about what is right and wrong. They are skilled at ascertaining what is feasible and practical as opposed to improbable and dangerous and, thus, not for you—thank you very much.

This Critic/Muse pair might show up when you are facing a decision— big or small. You might catch yourself caught between them when presented with an exciting but potentially risky possibility where you seek greater aliveness and freedom on the one hand but also security or predictability on the other. For example, "Should I quit my job or should I play it safe?" "Should I make a cross-country move now or should I wait until next year when I can be more prepared?" These two sides also can also be stimulated by commitments you made to yourself that you are tempted to break, such as, "Should I eat my salad for lunch or have this cookie instead?"

Our polarized parts can inform each other of their unique perspectives. The more polarized they appear, the more they might long for and benefit from connecting with each other's messages. Through dialogue, they can start to illuminate ways to work together for a higher good: your well-being.

AYDEN'S STORY:
TEAMWORK MAKES THE DREAM WORK

One of my first clients, Ayden, was feeling torn between the wishes of his Inner Critic and his Inner Muse. Ayden's Critic shouldered the pressures of working long hours for his job as an executive assistant, while his Muse craved time and freedom to devote to his own pursuits.

When he drew these figures, Ayden noticed that his Critic was a stiff stick-figure wearing glasses and carrying a briefcase, while his Muse was playfully grinning, depicted with a head of disheveled hair. Ayden felt that his Muse was unrestrained, free, and wild—a visionary who was willing to take risks. On the other hand, Ayden's Critic initially showed up as cautious, detail-oriented, and rigid in his desire to heed the rules and conform to external expectations.

In Ayden's dialogue below, his Muse—with whom Ayden identifies favorably—is bold, strong, and convincing. The Muse feels repressed by the Critic's sensible arguments. Rather than his two parts coming together with equal force, Ayden's emphatic Muse positively influences the Critic, softening him.

Sometimes, the exact opposite happens. When another client created her dialogue, her Muse was so buried that it was either silent or gave meek one-word answers. Her Critic, on the other hand, was so loud and prominent that upon encountering that all too-familiar voice, the client remarked, "That's just me!" It had been so long since she'd let herself dream that the Muse was not comfortable sharing yet.

In the cases where one part is silent or in the background, an encounter with another part can help show why it might be withdrawn. It may be a long path to arrive at an eventual middle ground, yet the meeting itself is a stepping stone. Instead of seeing one part as right and one as wrong, we can recognize that all our parts have wisdom and also blind spots which the other's perspective could illuminate.

Now, we will see Ayden work with his Muse and Critic in a colorful dialogue where they first converse about how to approach the topic of work-life balance.

—

Muse: Hi! How are you doing?

Critic: Fine.

Muse: You look a little upset. What's wrong?

Critic: I'm not upset, I've just got a lot to do, and there's no time to waste—what are we doing here?

Muse: Just having a team meeting, bro. Want to make sure we're all on the same page!

Critic: Okay, well, let's get it over with and get to it already.

Muse: What's the rush?

Critic: There's a lot to DO! A lot to work on!!

Muse: Why do you want to work on it? What are you trying to do?

Critic: To stay in good graces with everyone, we need to stay on top of things . . . , we need to stay on top of things. I've got the burden of doing all that while you are out enjoying the beach, so if you don't mind, I'll get back to work *(turns to shut the door)*.

Smiling, Muse goes in and picks up wet sand and smears it on the desk inside the cubicle.

Critic: What the hell? Why did you do that??

Muse: Life is messy! Stop trying to clean it up.

Critic: *(stunned, frustrated, angry, but getting a notion about something)* What do you mean?

Muse: The point of life isn't to stay in people's good graces. It's to make crazy confusing messes. Throw your paint on the canvas and turn it into something full of life. You are trying to keep it all spotless when the point is to put paint on it!

Critic's mind is working, his eyebrows squished as he tries to process this idea.

Muse: Let's talk out here!

Muse leads the way onto the beach and then sits next to the Critic.

Muse: Take your shoes off, put your feet in the sand.

Critic: Okaaay. . . .

Critic takes his shoes off, getting the tactile experience.

Muse: How does that feel?

Critic: This actually feels good. I've forgotten my feet could feel.

Muse: That might be true about more than just your feet.

Critic: Hmm, interesting.

Muse: Listen, Critic, we love what you do, and it is necessary to keep us on track, but if you don't share in the fun too, it is not good for you. We want you to reap the rewards and put your feet in the sand with us!

Critic: *(wanting to feel appreciated)* I don't believe that. You don't really like me. Sometimes I feel like a downer and that no one wants me around. . . .

Muse: You feel down because you're not around others and not enjoying your experiences. You've got it flipped—you'll feel more uplifted if you get around others more!

Critic is frozen in thought.

Muse: What do you think all of this is *for?*

Critic: I don't know. I am trying to stay afloat and keep my head above water.

Muse: Why are you only treading water? It's the ocean! Sometimes, you doggy paddle. Sometimes, you catch a wave! The point is to *swim.*

Critic: For so long, I've been trying to freeze myself into a certain way of being. I've been enforcing a plateau and stagnancy in my life to be "stable," but I don't want that at all—I hate that feeling! It makes me feel dead inside.

Muse: Yea, because life isn't something stable that you can control and hold together perfectly. The point is to ride the wave. What you are doing is valuable—you spot the roadblocks and potholes—but you can't spot them if you don't get in the car! You can make sure we have our seatbelts on, but first, you need to drive, or else you can't use your gifts.

Critic feels seen and understood. His body language shows he's less rigid and now more relaxed like a weight has been lifted off.

Muse: We've been waiting for you to come play with us! Now, would you climb out of that cubicle and have some fun?

Critic feels he belongs for once, rather than just trying to get others to like him.

Critic: Yea—I guess I don't need to go back to the cubicle for a while.

Muse hugs him and suddenly pushes him to the ground, then runs away laughing. Critic is covered in sand. His glasses fall off as he comes to grips with the messiness of life. Critic then gets up, and both go running off onto the beach, into new adventures!

As you can see from Ayden's story, the Muse may have been represented in a more extreme manner because the Critic was very trapped in its ways. Ayden's Critic was so critical that he was even beginning to doubt his own usefulness. When the Muse acknowledged the strengths and importance of the Critic, the Critic felt like it belonged and began to soften.

In more work with these two figures, the Critic agreed to put his tendency to focus on structure, form, and getting-things-done to good use and decided to take on a new name and role as The Architect. In his new role, rather than needing to follow things precisely step by step, he agreed to loosen the reins and enjoy the process of building Ayden's dreams.

In Ayden's story, we see that the idea is not to shut the Critic up nor get rid of him. Instead, it was to *include* him in a more balanced way. When Adyen's Critic became The Architect, this part could move from being rigid to helping Ayden place his awareness on his choices with intention and mindfulness. On the flip side, through further encounters, the Muse could also appreciate that The Architect's focus on stability could allow for more creativity and space within that structure.

Ayden's example illustrates how a protective part can learn to release its tight grip and find a new role that is more helpful. It can move from being defensive or disconnected to being of service. We will explore more about the Inner Critic and this kind of transformation in Chapter 6.

Now, by dialoguing with your own parts, you can get to know them each better and reveal their true intentions. You can help the parts who want to protect you find a productive way to do so. You can help the free-spirited dreamy parts shine without being careless. Just as Ayden experienced what he needed to see in that moment, your dialogue with your parts will reveal a helpful starting point.

CHAPTER 4 ACTIVITY:

Dialoguing with Different Parts

Now it is your turn to work with a duo inside you. In this activity, you will navigate an inner conflict to find the parts that need to connect with each other. You will craft a vivid inner dialogue to help illuminate their dynamic. This conversation between your seemingly opposed parts can lead to powerful insights into what you are really wanting, why, and what is in the way.

1) CHOOSE THE PLAYERS *(10 minutes)*

Choose two parts that seem at odds.

You can build on the previous chapters' activities by choosing the oppositional pair that you identified from your journaling in Chapter 1, your parts list from Chapter 2, or the opposed pair from your illustrations in Chapter 3. Referring to your parts map, you could choose two parts that you noticed have a discordant relationship.

Important: For this activity, do not select "wounded" or "shadow" parts or any parts that could be storing severe pain. We will not be covering those in this book and working with certain heavier parts could be best when accompanied by a resourced approach. This support can come from the Wise Self—whom we will meet in Chapter 7—or from the guidance of an experienced therapist who can create safety in navigating what gets stimulated.

If you are having trouble identifying which parts to work with, you can use this exercise to find them:

› Think of an upcoming decision or a place where you find yourself at a fork in the road. Any choice where you could hear a part of you say, "I want this" and then you hear another part chime in, "No way! We are *not* doing that!"

› First, imagine the part of you that is eager to live your vision. Is this part a Present part who wants to enjoy the beauties of life and take a vacation, a Nurturer who wants to bring new life into the world or get a pet, or maybe a Dreamer part who wants to climb Mt. Everest? Returning to your Chapter 2 exercise, see if you can identify this enthusiastic part with a name and some physical and personality characteristics. What qualities does this part embody?

› Take a few moments to relish the idea of bringing this visionary part's dreams into reality. What would you do if these wishes came true? Who would you be then?

› As you imagine this and expand your vision of the future, be aware of any hesitations or inner eye rolls. Notice any part of you that is doubting that this can be possible or who thinks that wealth, fame, joy, success, or freedom are for only the lucky few. After being in touch with your aspirational part, the one who is most in conflict with them should not be too hard to locate. Listen for the resistance or the concerns that pop up as you connect with those lofty dreams. This other part might start coming into view. As you hear its voice of resignation or skepticism, can you form a picture of this critical part?

› Allow yourself to see how tall this figure is, what their name is, and what expression they wear on their face. How are they feeling toward your dreams? What are their worries, their practical considerations, and the questions they want to pose, which seem to poke holes in your idealistic plans? What are their intentions in "bringing you back down to earth"?

2) **WRITE YOUR DIALOGUE** *(30 minutes)*

Next, with these figures in mind, as if writing a script, imagine they encounter each other. For example, a Muse could greet a Critic, starting with something simple such as, "Hi, how are you today?"

Write their dialogue out for at least 1-3 pages, letting your imagination and intuition guide what they say to each other. It is important to let this process unfold as if you are watching a movie or traveling inside a dream. Do not force outcomes or be tempted to impose your own solutions.

Tip: If you are more auditory, instead of writing, you can use a recording device to create an audio note of the conversation between the two parts. You can signal who is speaking each time by either changing your tone of voice or stating the part in advance of each new line.

3) **REFLECTION** *(15 minutes)*

> What did you learn when you did the exercise?

> What stands out to you as you review the dialogue?

> What did each part focus on?

> What did they each care most about?

> What insights did each part get from the other part?

> After this encounter, did you see any middle ground emerge that both sides could agree on?

> How can you apply these insights in your ideas and actions today?

CHAPTER 4 KEY CONCEPTS

› Parts can be strong-willed. Two specific parts can often be in staunch opposition to each other, creating an inner battle.

› Parts that appear opposed are often actually most in need of connecting with each other's messages. Both have valuable perspectives to share but may be blocking each other's wisdom from reaching you.

› When polarized parts get a chance to relate to one another, that encounter may reveal valuable insights about your inner world and the dynamics that are longing to shift.

› One example of a typical conflicted pair is your Muse and your Critic. Ever the creative optimist, the Muse has grand ideas and wants to leap into action without necessarily thinking it through. At the same time, the Critic can overthink things, spiraling into self-doubt and skepticism, prioritizing caution over adventure.

› Facilitating dialogue between two parts can illuminate their dynamic and shed light on why you might sometimes feel stuck.

› Sometimes, through parts' dialoguing, resolution or insight can come immediately, while other times, the basic connection is the next step that makes a later solution possible. The key is just to cultivate a relationship and get the parts to connect with each other.

› Helping your opposing parts to understand each other helps you to understand yourself. From this new perspective, you can gain a richer appreciation for these apparently competing voices and release the burden of your inner struggle.

› With more inner agreement, you will more easily be able to prioritize what matters most to you.

> Letting parts encounter each other through conversation can help them resolve their conflicts and illuminate new options, opportunities, and direction for you.

> This chapter's dialoguing activity can provide clues as to how to make your visions come to fruition in a way that feels aligned for all parts of you.

EMBRACING YOUR PARTS' NEEDS AND MESSAGES

Move from Resistance to Acceptance

The Guest House

This being human is a guest house.
Every morning a new arrival.

A joy, a depression, a meanness,
some momentary awareness comes
as an unexpected visitor.

Welcome and entertain them all!
Even if they are a crowd of sorrows,
who violently sweep your house
empty of its furniture,
still, treat each guest honorably.
He may be clearing you out
for some new delight.

The dark thought, the shame, the malice,
meet them at the door laughing,
and invite them in.

Be grateful for whoever comes.
because each has been sent
as a guide from beyond.

— RUMI (TRANSLATION BY COLEMAN BARKS)

This Rumi poem concludes that our visiting emotions are "sent as a guide from beyond," but in the context of parts, it could also say, "Each has been sent as a guide *from within*." In either case, this classic poem illustrates a compassionate stance we can take to our own humanity. It suggests that we can treat all our experiences as honorable guests in the home of our being. Whether they initially seem courteous or disruptive, these guests may even end up becoming our teachers.

We will now approach your emotions and parts with curiosity and openness to learn from each of them. In the last chapter, we saw how parts dialoguing with each other revealed their dynamic points of view. In this chapter, we will explore how cultivating the willingness to understand your parts allows you to uncover their underlying needs and receive the gifts they want to share with you. You will gain deeper self-acceptance as you learn to listen to your parts, helping them to become more effective team players within you.

THE SKY HOLDS
ALL THE WEATHER

Often, as we encounter our parts, we realize that we like some of them more than others. There are those we welcome, ones we might consider "sunny"—who seem bright, useful, or positive. Conversely, we shun and resist parts that are seemingly less desirable—"stormier" parts who are jealous or nitpicky and which we judge as bad, despicable, or annoying.

The inner sunbeams, the lightning, or the hail that make up our internal landscape are all equally parts of the fabric of our being. By beginning to cultivate a space of pure awareness, we can nonjudgmentally view our internal weather as part of our nature.

The sky allows every form of weather to dance across its expanse, even as it changes moment to moment. By permitting your internal weather to pass through the vastness of your awareness, your parts and their emotions will feel more welcome to share their messages with you. This accepting approach is the medicine that makes parts work so transformative.

Without attaching to our parts or overidentifying with any of them, we can still recognize that all of them are essential players in our inner ecosystem. As long as we remain open, it is easier to sail through the storms stimulated by these trickier aspects of ourselves.

Like someone with the best of intentions for us, our parts believe what they are doing is the most effective way to offer support. Of course, if they are out of touch with the whole picture, their efforts can cause more strife than anything else. While it is true that all our parts deserve a seat at the table, if you feel under-resourced, then maybe these visitors are initially welcome for tea but don't need to spend the night.

Additionally, though all our parts are essential players in our inner tapestry, they are not always equally present. In different moments, some parts are more tangible and have a greater need for your loving attention than others. In stormy moments, you may know the sun is there, but it is hidden from view. Thus, you would be most focused on getting an umbrella to address the immediate concern of the rain. Likewise, you can usually work most easily with the parts that are "up" for you at any given time while remembering that the others are still on deck, awaiting their turn.

We can be open to working with all of our parts when the time is right, trusting that our loving attention and the passage of time will support them in contributing to our growth. Through being accepted, our parts can all organically come into the right relationship with what is needed for the full self. Of course, this shift often occurs when we stop trying to make our parts something they are not and start to genuinely understand them. It is a paradox: when we want something to change, it tends to stay the same, and when we accept it as it is, it feels free to transform.

ACCEPTANCE AS LISTENING

When we talk about acceptance here, it does not mean giving up or defaulting to a suboptimal reality. Accepting ourselves is not about being resigned to "less than," condoning unhealthy behaviors, wallowing, or indulging in your favorite self-pity party. Acceptance also does not mean tolerating endless heartbreak or suffering through struggles. You can accept parts of you without agreeing with or acquiescing to their initial viewpoints, especially when those are coming from pain and potentially skewed.

True acceptance is an active process of willingly listening for the underlying truth of "what is." It means opening to the vulnerability of sensing where our hearts have closed. It means choosing to meet the obstacles that arise and see each moment through to the other side. Staying the course can allow you to locate the tender need that has been asking for your attention. Touching the truth of what your parts care about can restore you to the beautiful core underneath it all.

When we choose to look for the lessons, messages, and teachings from inside the darkness, our challenges can sometimes offer us an invitation to grow. Our experiences, even the less appealing ones, can become part of our evolution. Thus, our "undesirable" parts can be seen as a road map to our tenderness. In the process of acceptance, we allow our parts to take a seat at the table, when we are ready to greet them. We trust that by listening to their messages, we can uncover deeper truths.

When you start trusting in the value of your parts, you may find that behind the fear or worry they carry is something precious. Underneath what is *scared* in you is what is **sacred** to you. Our fearful parts may be pointing to what matters most to us, showing us we don't want to lose it. Fear can also show us our edges by telling us when it is safest to stop or pause. Or, fear can even reveal our desire to develop skills so that we can be empowered in the face of what previously hurt us. In a similar way, jealousy—another "undesirable" feeling or part—can often be a window into what we desire and shows us our longing to trust that we can create what we see others have created. Thus, our more challenging emotions and parts can act as a compass, signaling what is important to us.

In many cases, our shunned parts are the ones that contain the greatest gifts. Since these parts can be the most sensitive and thus vulnerable, we hide them, even though they are likely to house our superpowers! When we create an environment for all our parts to feel safe and comfortable enough to reveal themselves, then they can be who they truly are and act in accordance with their most authentic intentions. In that way, we can let go of anything that is no longer serving us, and make space for a new way of being.

By truly understanding each part of you, you will no longer want to get rid of them; instead, you will want to embrace their true nature and treat them with compassion, unconditional love, and gentle care.

TRANSFORMATION THROUGH ACCEPTANCE

The chart that follows helps illustrate how acceptance creates transformation. We can attend to parts that need *self-preservation* (meeting essential needs) as well as *self-expression* (sharing oneself through creativity).

STARTING POINT: INNER STRUGGLE (AIM: SELF-PRESERVATION)		TRANSFORMS INTO ⇒ INTEGRATED STATE (AIM: SELF-ACTUALIZATION)
› **Self-Doubt**	**It looks like . . .**	**Self-Awareness.**
› You feel a nagging force that instills fear.	› You feel stuck in worry mode.	› You can explore without jumping to conclusions or getting ahead of yourself.
› You are overprotective and armed against big changes.	› stressed, confused, conflicted, and full of misgivings.	› You can get to know yourself without judgment and with compassion.
› You come up with reasons you will fail and should not try.	› You are not aware of the strength of your true nature (which contains wisdom, freedom, and resilience).	› You meet your reality with curiosity and an eagerness to learn.
› You make excuses for maintaining the status quo.		› You prepare as necessary and can imagine wonderful possibilities emerging instead of fixating on the worst-case scenario.
› You think:	› You feel disconnected from the larger picture (from nature, faith, community, and your inherent value).	
› "I can't."		› You are open to growth, truth, and being led.
› "I shouldn't."		› You hold a sense of trust and lean into insight that can emerge from understanding.
› "What if [terrible thing] happens?"		› When the nagging doubts and fretful fears turn into constructive observation, a self-aware state offers a pragmatic and grounded perspective that helps you grow.

STARTING POINT: INNER STRUGGLE (AIM: SELF-PRESERVATION)		TRANSFORMS INTO ⇒ INTEGRATED STATE (AIM: SELF-ACTUALIZATION)
Self-Judgment/ Judgment	**It looks like . . .**	**Self-Acceptance/ Acceptance**
› You are full of dissatisfaction and criticism for yourself or others:	› Thoughts arise that you (and anything you do) are not good enough.	› You truly love your *whole* self, not just the parts you view as good.
› "*I'm* not enough."	› You berate yourself for any mistakes or for missing the mark.	› You welcome yourself and others with open arms and sincere warmth.
› "*It's* not enough."		
› "*You're* not enough."		
› You feel unhappy and discontent with yourself, others, and your life circumstances.	› You always demand more from yourself.	› You see the gems of wisdom and usefulness of parts you used to judge.
› You resist taking action because the thing you are creating isn't perfect.	› You shrink back or draw inward.	› You can *discern* what is best for you without necessarily making someone, something else, or yourself "wrong."
› You hide under the pretense of high standards, which paralyzes forward movement.	› This state of judgment might induce feelings of inadequacy, jealousy, resentment, and worthlessness.	› The uncertain and skeptical parts reveal their true desires of wanting you to be emotionally safe, feel accepted, and belong.
		› With self-acceptance, you begin to belong to yourself first. Then connection with others follows from that secure love.

STARTING POINT: INNER STRUGGLE (AIM: SELF-PRESERVATION)		TRANSFORMS INTO ⇒ INTEGRATED STATE (AIM: SELF-ACTUALIZATION)
Self-Conscious/ Constricted	**It looks like . . .**	**Self-Expression**
› You are reserved.	› You feel awkward and uncomfortable in your own skin.	› You see the reserved parts of you as being mindful of needs like belonging and acceptance.
› Your cautious parts hold you back.	› You assume you are imposing on others, are a burden, or are doing something "wrong."	› You find belonging by being authentic and giving your gifts.
› You feel shaky and uncertain about how you might appear to others and concerned about what they might think of you.	› You shy away from sharing yourself with others and the world.	› You choose to share, shine, create, and sing your heart out simply because you have a song inside that you trust yourself enough to share.
› You prejudge yourself so that you can beat others to the punch.		› You feel a strong purpose or reason to participate and that your voice matters.
		› You are connected to the contribution you can make by being who you are.
		› You express your gifts, not just for you but also for the benefit of others.
		› The tentative fear of how you might affect others negatively becomes an awareness of the power of your presence and a feeling of joy at being able to make a positive impact.

A Chinese proverb echoes this theme of acceptance: "Tension is who you think you should be. Relaxation is who you are."

Instead of imposing expectations on ourselves that lead to constriction, we can learn to meet our parts in the moment lovingly. We can identify these "shoulding" voices and understand which insights they have for us rather than rebelling against them or buckling under their pressure. In doing so, we allow for possibilities greater than what we might hope for or expect.

SURRENDER WHAT DOES NOT SERVE: ALLOW THE NOW

Be crumbled. So wildflowers will come up where you are. You have been stony for too many years. Try something different. Surrender.

— RUMI

As we allow our feelings to be as they are, we surrender to exactly what is there. In this context, surrender does not mean waving a white flag and giving up. Surrender means to soften, make space, allow, and be willing to be led. As we surrender, we give up the resistance that keeps us from connecting with reality and staying with it. We are not surrendering to our parts but rather surrendering our resistance toward our parts.

Surrendering through acceptance doesn't mean complacence, laziness, or indulgence in a victim mindset. Rather, it is a gateway to connecting with our precious needs and finding more powerful ways to meet them. Surrender means opening to all of our parts and letting them teach us what we need to learn so we can heal and grow. In this way, we can continue to become the strong, whole, and loving people that we have been all along.

Connecting with our present emotions or parts paradoxically allows them to return to their true nature—one that has until now been obscured. Our emotions can prove valuable indicators of our truth, craving an outlet to express themselves. When we trust that we are big enough to hold them all, we will not see our emotions or parts as good or bad, and we will not have the urge to run from any of them.

NEEDS AND STRATEGIES

As you continue connecting to your parts, you will identify their needs, desires, and messages. This process applies to parts you may be resisting that may simply be trying to communicate something important. It also applies to interacting with parts you find likable but that may be in the background or taken for granted. You will get to see more nuance in each part as you allow them to reveal their true colors.

We can approach our inner selves with compassion by employing conflict resolution tools similar to those presented in psychologist Marshall Rosenberg's work. Rosenberg's writings on empathic communication offer a way to relate that emphasizes truth, authenticity, connection, and intentionality. In his landmark book, *Nonviolent Communication*, Rosenberg distinguishes between the actual things we think and do (ex: giving a gift to a friend) and the needs those actions and strategies meet (ex: contribution to another's well-being). Rosenberg suggests that as we understand the needs we are trying to meet through our actions, we can find better ways to meet those needs.

For example, if you judge your brother as lazy and call him that, you may be doing so because you are trying to motivate him to help with the dishes. However, once you recognize that you want support, you may find less combative—and more effective—ways to meet that need. You might request a shared cleaning schedule or agree to be responsible for the dishes if he assumes the duty of taking out the trash.

In the context of parts, your parts' needs might be satisfied by a variety of *different* strategies, not just the one you think of initially and to which you might have become attached. The solutions we first conceive of are not necessarily as effective as ones we could devise if we took time to connect to the underlying needs.

For example, your Overwhelmed Olga part may suggest that eating three handfuls of your favorite cookies is an easy way to meet your need for comfort. However, Fitness Focused Francesca might be less than enthused by this splurge, given her aspirations toward healthier living. By recognizing that they want both comfort and health, you might find a creative way to fulfill these needs for soothing and self-care, perhaps by taking a bubble bath and savoring one cookie without feeling guilty. By listening for what your system really longs for, your parts have a chance to agree on harmonious strategies that will not be counterproductive in the long term.

When a part is overtaking you with its own agenda, it often becomes louder when you have not listened in a meaningful way to what it wants. This part may swiftly resort to the solution it believes will quickly satisfy its need, even if this approach comes at a cost to other needs. When you pay attention to that part, you can connect it to your larger inner system and make a more deliberate decision that considers all aspects.

When we approach our undesired feelings or parts with an energy of fixing them, dealing with them, or even changing them, our stance is already laced with intolerance. Some part of us is using judgment as an attempt to identify what is not working. However, when we can accept all our parts, we can empathically *discern* what they each need. We realize that if the part knew a better, easier, or more feasible way to meet its needs, it would. This understanding applies just as much to the parts who are doing the judging!

From the dialogue examples in Chapter 4, you might have noticed that even parts in conflict are just doing the best they can with what they know. Some tend to lean toward fear habitually, so the *way* they go about serving you might not be ideal. However, in witnessing the dialogues between parts, you could see how their interactions revealed more than initially met the eye. By applying the tools in this chapter, you will open to your parts' specific messages, connect with the inherent goodness of their intentions, and see them as allies.

—

Now, let's explore Sebastian's story to see how meeting your parts with acceptance allows transformation. Here, Sebastian toes the line between self-indulgence (wallowing with no movement as there is a sense of resistance) and self-compassion (meeting what is true within himself with loving acceptance). Two different parts of him illustrate the pushpull he feels within. Once Sebastian takes time to understand both his parts' needs better, he can make room for them to express their useful intentions.

SEBASTIAN'S STORY: TUNING
IN INSTEAD OF TUNING OUT

Sebastian had moved back home to job search following his unemployment. Two sides of him were at odds as he tried to motivate himself. On the one hand, he had a Lazy Brain who just wanted to chill. This part lived by the motto, "Oh, I have plennntyy of time . . . " On the other hand, he felt the aggressive energy of what he called Anxious Brain who pressured him to churn out cover letters and resumes. This fretful part badgered him with thoughts like, "What are you *doing*?? *What* do you have to show for yourself?"

Since his former job had been very demanding, Sebastian needed time to himself to rest and breathe. However, anytime he was not productive, he was very hard on himself. We entered an exploration to meet both these parts and find a harmonious way forward that incorporated the underlying wisdom of each.

We began by taking stock of Sebastian's current inner world.

Jeanine: What do Lazy Brain and Anxious Brain want you to know— what do they each feel is true?

Lazy Brain: I have plenty of time. It is okay to relax! I am bouncing back, so I am entitled to do whatever I want. I am in a supported environment, so I do not have to stress. There do not seem to be many jobs in my field right now, so why bother?

Anxious Brain: I cannot live like this! Lounging around is suffocating! Why are you idling? You have to do more than this! You have to grow up and get out of this environment. I feel stunted here. I want you to learn more, do more, be more. *You're not doing enough.* What are you going to do about money? You are going to lose everything and be stuck here forever! That is not an option. We cannot live like this!

Lazy Brain freezes, not knowing what to do. He suddenly feels disorganized and dazed in his thinking.

Lazy Brain: Now it feels like someone is watching my every move and micromanaging me!

Anxious Brain gets more frustrated and more intense. He feels backed into a corner and wants to throw a temper tantrum.

Anxious Brain: Stop acting like a deer in headlights!

I stepped in to speak with the parts directly.

Jeanine to Anxious Brain: You think Sebastian is stagnating, and that must feel frustrating. What do you need him to do to trust that all is headed in a good direction?

Anxious Brain: Action! I need some degree of action, even if it is small. I want to feel that Sebastian is putting the work in and getting things done (rather than choosing Lazy Brain's side all the time and just putting his feet up)!

Sebastian to Anxious Brain: I am trying, but I am feeling lost and stuck, and I am not sure how much time it will all take. I cannot guarantee this will be a quick process. We might need to follow a meandering path for a while until it all comes together.

Jeanine to Lazy Brain: Why don't you want to move forward? Why are you feeling better about staying still?

Lazy Brain: I feel It is better just to sit back because I do not want to put myself out on the chopping block. I have already gotten rejected from all the jobs I have applied to so far. I do not want to risk more failure.

Sebastian commented that this helped to explain his procrastinating tendencies. He would put things off (via Lazy Brain) until the other part of him got fed up. Anxious Brain would then slam the accelerator in any direction, just to be reassured there was movement. He would send out a flurry of applications just before the deadlines but didn't trust he had put enough time and effort to put his best foot forward.

Since Sebastian was open to learning more about both parts, next we inquired into their underlying needs to see if they wanted to reveal their truer intentions for Sebastian.

Lazy Brain: I am advocating for a sense of ease and comfort. I want Sebastian to experience stability and security, and I only know how to help him feel that by hitting pause on everything.

Sebastian: Thank you, Lazy Brain. I do need that very much. However, I want to find a way to give us that relief without it derailing my progress.

Lazy Brain: It feels good to be acknowledged. I would like to become "The ReFueler" and help you rest so you can recharge.

Anxious Brain: And I want Sebastian to have an outlet to feel passionate, engrossed, capable, and powerful, in addition to feeling relaxed. I'm tired of relaxation taking over everything else!

Sebastian: Thank you, Anxious Brain. I appreciate your tireless efforts to help move things forward. Without that, I don't know where I'd be, so thanks for that push. I want to take concrete action steps in a good direction, just without feeling frenetic and pressured about it!

Anxious Brain: I can be "The Expander" for you, so you can pursue your potential and realize that of which you are capable!

Sebastian: *(after we debriefed)* Wow, it felt good to dig into that. That needed some major digging!

From Sebastian's example, we can see that life presents us with the dance between our desire to be more and our desire to be enough. It is great to ask ourselves, "What's next?" However, it is also important to evolve without making the desire for more mean that we are not enough right now.

Sebastian learned to make an important distinction between true rest and laziness. While his procrastination was a form of worry or fear in disguise, taking quality time off to himself allowed him to reset and ultimately be more productive as well. When Sebastian could consult his pushing part (Anxious Brain), he was more able to use his free time to **tune in** by paying attention rather than **tune out** by distracting himself.

Rather than simply bingeing TV shows and feeling sullen about "wasting time," Sebastian was able to choose to recharge through meditation, walking his dog mindfully, and cooking. When Sebastian permitted himself to rest when he needed it, he realized that even watching TV shows is not a bad way to relax. What made it beneficial or detrimental depended on the number of shows he would consume. The quantity and his approach made the difference between fun entertainment and mindless indulgence. Like the difference between medicine and poison, the key was in the dosage. After our work together, Sebastian said he felt freer to take the space he needed to decompress with less guilt. The guilt was a signal that the motivating part (Anxious Brain) was not getting its needs met. Once Sebastian found a good balance between rest and work that fully honored each in their time, the guilt subsided.

As you can see from this example, pushing parts try to motivate you, but when they become extreme in their approach, it can backfire. When you do not take the rest you need, then one part of you might forcefully take that time anyway. However, this impulsive or rebellious move may have the side effect of another part feeling ashamed about your inaction, thwarting any feelings of rejuvenation from the downtime. You might feel this inner tension when only one part's needs are getting met rather than coming up with a solution or approach that works for both. Like Sebastian, we can learn to find our natural ebbs and honor them with rest. And when we are in a flow, we can take the right next steps that feel aligned, carrying them out with presence and dedication.

ALYSSA'S WALL OF FEELINGS:
FROM PROTECTION TO CONNECTION

*Your task is not to seek for love, but merely to
seek and find all the barriers within yourself
that you have built against it.*

— RUMI

In our next example, we will see what unfolded for Alyssa when she worked with undesired parts that showed up as dark feelings. These uncomfortable emotions wanted her attention and were in the driver's seat until Alyssa shifted from resistance to acceptance.

Alyssa had done work in therapy around navigating her relationship with her mother, who was often self-absorbed and inattentive. Alyssa came to understand that she had a hard time trusting that people cared about her from her experience of feeling abandoned growing up. Even though it was an old belief, the thoughts of not being good enough remained.

When I initially met her, a mandatory shelter-in-place order had kept Alyssa home for a month. As a single woman without pets or any solitary hobbies, she was feeling lonely. She mentioned that, before quarantine, she had healthy outlets for her energy, such as socializing with friends, going to the gym, and visiting the beach. However, now she felt that she was spinning and thinking entirely of negative things. Alyssa commented, "I feel really needy—and I *hate* that feeling." Though Alyssa usually had a calm, composed, and kind demeanor, the effects of the lockdown were getting to her.

On the day that we spoke, Alyssa was feeling sad about feeling forgotten and a part of her was trying to defend against that pain. "I'm on a kick of not wanting to care what others think of me. I've done that my whole life and am getting sick of it." Still, she did care. She felt hurt that her friends were not checking in on her during this challenging time, yet she didn't know how to deal with those emotions. She mentioned that she found herself reacting negatively to a seemingly small event. A good friend of hers had randomly sent her a funny image that was an inside joke between them, but Alyssa noticed resentment creep up instead of feeling the connection she wanted. She wished her friend would take the time to call her directly instead of texting something seemingly frivolous. Alyssa understood that her friend was busy with her children, but she still longed for the deeper connection that a phone call would provide. A part of her felt that if her friend was not calling, she must not care.

Reflecting on her experience, Alyssa remarked, "Why do I doubt that my close friends love me? These people *tell* me they care about me! Am I feeling this way because I have nothing else to do and am going stir crazy?"

Alyssa wondered if she was feeling abandoned because the people in her life were not thoughtful enough or if she felt this way because of something she was thinking or doing. On the one hand, it would be hard to admit that some of her struggles were self-created. On the other hand, taking responsibility for what she had the agency to change could be empowering.

The pain of this realization inspired Alyssa's determination to have a better relationship with herself and others. If she was feeling hurt, annoyed, or angry with someone, she resolved not to lose control over her emotions, which she said usually tended to get the best of her. Instead, she was willing to look within first.

When she came to our session, one of her big questions was, *"How can I not be so negative right now?"* So, we began an exploration where I guided Alyssa to connect more with her underlying feelings and needs.

———

Jeanine: How do you feel about how you feel?

Alyssa: I think these are ugly emotions. I want a better relationship with myself so I am not upset at others and not keeping score about who is reaching out or not. I don't want to get so offended.

Jeanine: What needs do you have that are feeling unmet?

Alyssa: Mattering, significance, and consideration.

Jeanine: Have you communicated to anyone that you are feeling lonely?

Alyssa: I don't want to verbalize it because I don't trust them to hold it. Yesterday, the guy I've been dating called me when he had only a few minutes to speak, and I missed the call. There went our ten minute window to speak. Rather than thinking, "It's nice he's trying to talk to me when he has a moment free," the scared part of me is feeling like he is only squeezing me in to appease me and that I am not a priority for him.

Alyssa: *(reflecting on these feelings, sighing)* What is wrong with me right now? I'm scrutinizing it all!

Jeanine: What is the story you are telling yourself about all this?

Alyssa: The story I am telling myself is that nobody cares or loves me enough or as much as I love them. Also, I feel there is this huge part of me that is always preparing for rejection, and then it becomes a selffulfilling prophecy because I am always worrying about that and focusing on it.

When she felt overrun by this victim mentality, Alyssa's coping strategy was to back off and withdraw completely. It was as if she had a wall of anger up to defend against the vulnerable feelings underneath.

*As she was speaking, I wondered, "What if the parts of Alyssa that think that **others** aren't loving her are actually crying out for **her** to love them?"*

From there, we started a dialogue between Alyssa and the feelings inside herself that she was resisting and labeling as negative.

Jeanine: Imagine you are on one side of a wall, and all the stuff you dislike about yourself is on the other side.

Alyssa: It is a clear wall, like a glass or a mirror.

Jeanine: On the other side are all the words representing the feelings you have that you don't like. What are they?

Alyssa: Resentment. Mistrust. Abandonment. Worry. Anxiety. Ugly. They pop up as big black words in sloppy cursive writing.

I noticed a slight pause and a shift in her tone.

Jeanine: What's coming up for you?

Alyssa: *(in tears)* These words feel real! It's like they are me! I identify with these things that are negative—and bad! That's *me*.

Alyssa: *(continuing)* It's a part of me I don't want to see. I don't want to be those things or treat other people that way.

Jeanine: Perhaps the person that these words are affecting the most is you. Take a moment to let the words know how you feel about them.

Alyssa: *(addressing her feelings directly)* I don't want to feel this way. You make my chest hurt, and you make time go slowly. You are in my head and body too much, and it's useless. This doesn't create good lasting relationships, and I don't want to feel this way. I want you to go away. I don't want you to just go somewhere where you get suppressed, I want you to just go away, and I want to learn how to get rid of you in a healthy way.

Jeanine: Because if you go away . . .

Alyssa: If you go away, then I will be *happy*! I'll be content, able to treat others with respect, and will be able to believe other people. I won't have this constant feeling of people being out to get me.

Jeanine: Which makes me feel . . .

Alyssa: Which makes me feel that I can't trust or believe their intentions. It makes me feel like I just don't believe they really care about me. So, I get tight inside like I'm constantly defending myself. It's a feeling that nobody cares—that people care more about their own lives and don't genuinely care about me.

Jeanine: Which must mean . . .

Alyssa: *(without hesitation)* Which must mean that I'm not important.

Jeanine: And I want to trust instead . . .

Alyssa: I want to trust that what people tell me is the truth and that I can rest in that they care about me. They show me that I matter to them, and I want to receive their actual love.

Jeanine: Which would make me feel . . .

Alyssa: Content, at peace, happy. I would just know, and there'd be this feeling inside me that either way, I am still okay. No matter what they think, feel, and do, I am okay inside.

Jeanine: How are the words now?

Alyssa: They are smaller, and rather than popping up in front of me, they are going backward.

Jeanine: What else is happening?

Alyssa: *(with an easeful sigh)* It feels like there is space now. I see myself sitting in front of that mirror, and I feel glad that I got all that out! Rather than all those big loud words, I only see myself there. I feel more relaxed and less tight. I don't feel like I need to do anything or go anywhere. I just am.

Jeanine: I am . . .

Alyssa: I am okay. I am calm.

Jeanine: How do you feel now toward your friend who sent the funny text message from this space?

Alyssa: I feel just fine toward her. I don't have any bad feelings towards her. I just feel regular towards her. If I saw her right now, I would give her a hug.

Jeanine: How do you feel toward the man you are dating from this space?

Alyssa: I feel okay about him too. I recognize that we are both doing the best that we can. There's no more confusion or anger, just a feeling of either way this will be okay.

When we understand that our relationship with ourselves often mirrors our relationship with others, it can give us a renewed sense of agency. When Alyssa was being hard on others, it was because she was being hard on herself. When she had compassion for herself, she felt better about others in her life too.

Initially, Alyssa made unspoken demands of others to fill her needs for love and affection in specific ways and timeframes. Once she began to connect with these needs and address them within herself, Alyssa found she could more freely receive and give love in various forms. From here, we continued to learn more about the true source of her emotions.

Jeanine: What did those words really want you to know? What would they say to you?

Alyssa: They would say, "We want you to know that we are trying to make you see the whole story. We are trying to protect you by making sure that you can look at things from two different sides. We want you to know that you don't need to be scared of us. There's a positive way to look at situations, trusting that your best interest is held at heart. But, on the flip side, we also want to protect you from when people might hurt you."

Jeanine: How do you respond to those emotions now?

Alyssa: *(to the feelings)* I see now that you are there because my loved ones have hurt me before, so thank you for trying to be there for me and protect me and make me see different aspects of the situation. Maybe next time, could you not be so intense? Just be there for me. There's a part of me that wants to trust you, knowing you are here for me. But you don't need to be so out of control and all-consuming! Let's remember that it's still okay, and the people in my life are not villains.

Like Alyssa, sometimes we do not like the way our parts first appear. We tackle some parts like they are to be exchanged with something better as soon as possible. When we feel this resistance, a part of us is essentially telling other parts that they are not good, not useful, or not okay as they are. Yet, so much of our inner conflict is perpetuated because, as the saying goes, "What we resist persists!" Since we may be scared to be vulnerable, we may avoid looking at what is really going on within ourselves. We might turn to distractions—drowning ourselves in work, exercise, television, or even more unhealthy diversions.

Often, it is not the part (or the negative feeling) itself that is causing trouble as much as our own resistance or judgmental feelings toward that part. Basically, we feel bad; then we feel bad *about* feeling bad! On some level, we are communicating to ourselves that what's happening is unacceptable and intolerable. So we do not face it head-on for fear of touching the tenderness, grief, and pain that may arise if we stand still for a moment to listen.

For Alyssa, when she took time to pause and listen to these "negative" emotions, she unveiled the unmet needs that they were trying to signal to her.

As we see illustrated here, acceptance is an approach of meeting reality with kindness and with the desire to see, hear, and feel the truth. In

Alyssa's case, taking time to listen to the messages from her unwanted feelings helped her to soften. She came to understand her deep longing for love and affection and release her expectations around how these should be expressed. Through working with her emotions, Alyssa became aware of how she was defending herself against receiving those feelings because, on some level, she felt mistrustful. By remembering that she was loved by others and by giving herself some self-compassion, she became more open to letting love in—both from herself and those around her.

Like Alyssa did here, we can take the time to connect with our authenticity as the doorway to inner freedom. This brave confrontation with our truth becomes the medicine for our ailing parts. Every part is needed and welcome. If a part is arising in us, then we trust that it has a function and contains an insight that will only be revealed when we honor its contribution without resistance.

ALLOWING YOUR PARTS TO SHINE

Since you do not resist or dislike all your parts, some will be easier to embrace than others. Working to accept the intentions of challenging parts teaches us to embrace their underlying valuable messages. Other times, we identify with or enjoy certain parts, but we have not gotten to know them as well, or we perhaps feel shy to let them share their most vibrant expression. Working with these parts helps us to liberate our gifts. Even if you think you already accept a part and approve of them, you can still inquire into their deeper messages, get to know them better, and listen to them in their fullness.

Even the parts that do not create friction inside you still have more to share, and as you explore the next activity, you will gain an appreciation for their unique roles. When you do not inquire more deeply, the parts may seem stereotypical or like caricatures of themselves. By listening to their messages and approaching them with a willingness to hear what they have to say, you appreciate the nuances of their personalities as they reveal different dimensions of themselves.

THE DANCE OF LIFE

While it was always rich to work with parts that I resisted or who were in conflict, I also found tremendous value working with parts that already evoked resonance and inspiration. In this next example, I will share about how getting to know my Dancer part allowed me to gain insight into new ways to approach life. As I connected with this part and recognized her value, I allowed her greater freedom to show herself in the world.

I have always loved to dance—from ballet to figure skating, bhangra to salsa dancing, and even yoga dance! I love the freedom and fluidity that this form of expression gives. When I illustrated my Dancer, I saw how this part allowed me to experience grace in movement. Dancing allowed me to lead in terms of choosing motions and feeling empowered. Yet, perhaps more importantly, dance also invited me to *follow* as I was responding to the music, a dance partner, or my own emotions that were expressed through my movement.

Following the activity from Chapter 2 of illustrating a part, I made the following painting of my free-spirited Dancer part in 2010:

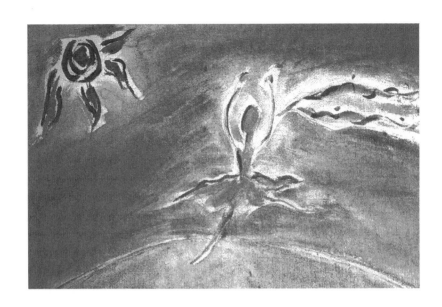

Years later, the following photo was taken of me on a beach in Mexico:

When I saw these images side by side one day, it clicked! I saw the resemblance, down to the arc of my posture and the ribbon in the air. My jaw dropped open as I realized I had stepped into living this part in the world.

From the beginning, I already appreciated this part and loved being able to express this side of me. However, getting to hear her speak further strengthened my connection to her. I used the following prompts which you will explore at the end of this chapter to invite the Dancer part to share. Here were my Dancer's responses to this self-inquiry:

> *My biggest fear is . . .* you holding back who you truly are out of fear of not being accepted or intimidating someone.

> *My deepest desire for you is . . .* to shine your light for others and for yourself.

> *My unique strength is . . .* moving through all things that arise in life—the joyful moments as well as the tough ones.

> *I want you to know . . .* that you are allowed to take up space and that your joy is a gift, not a signal of ignorance.

> *A message I have for you today is . . .* when you dance freely, it could even inspire others to join in, and you could spark a celebration!

In addition, I was inspired by a key prompt they use in the SoulCollage® process. Contemplating the perspective of any of your parts, you can write freely from their vantage point, beginning with the sentence stem: *"I Am The One Who . . . "*

For my Dancer, here is what flowed from connecting with her message:

The Dancer: *"I am the One Who . . . "*

I am the One Who dances your joy, giving it life
I am the One Who moves you through your stagnation and your grief
I am the One Who teaches you how to bow and bend
I stay too; there is stillness even in my movement

I teach you to rise and reach UP
like tree roots in the pavement who are still in love with heaven
I teach you to ground down as well
like when birds land on the earth and feel the grass tickle their feathers

I am the One Who allows everything to be what it is, as it is
I am the One Who chooses to answer to the rhythm no one else is
listening to

I am the One Who follows what arises with a flowing "YES"
I am the One Who meets every moment as my dance partner
And I am the One Who rests in the movement of life

—

In reflecting on these writings, I saw that the Dancer part is not just
a physical part that likes to move around, whether on a ballroom
floor or a beach. Through this activity, she revealed how she is much
vaster than I imagined. Her words expressed how much she embod-
ies the metaphorical dance of life. She also emphasized how dancing
is my medicine for hard moments and becomes my joyful gift in
happy times.

Connecting with this part has become a portal to my vibrancy and
authenticity since through dancing, I allow my emotions to flow
instead of staying stuck. In listening to the Dancer's message, I gained
deeper appreciation of her nuances and gifts. By connecting with
vibrant parts that spark your creativity and joy, you can expand these
uplifting qualities in yourself, and your life!

Now, in this chapter's activity, we will look at what happens when you allow each of your parts to share something with you. Using the prompts at the end of this chapter, you will get to ask your parts about their needs and desires to connect with their valuable perspectives. You can help each by letting them know they are welcome to share, as you whole-heartedly embrace both the likable ones and the ones toward which you feel resistance.

CHAPTER 5 ACTIVITY:

"I Want You to Know"

In the activity to follow, you will listen for the deeper truth behind the parts you seem to like and the ones you do not. You will embrace each of your parts and listen for their valuable messages and needs. In doing so, you will take steps to dust off the diamond that is you, revealing the brilliant shine of your original self, one with many facets!

In relating to the parts that are most alive for you today, you can cultivate a loving attention that gives them the space to express themselves more fully.

Reminder: Respect your own threshold for what you can handle, and seek support if things seem too overwhelming to manage. In some cases, you may even want a guide to work with parts that surface resentment, anger, or pain. To anchor the space in true acceptance, you might cultivate a connection with an external mentor or teacher or choose to invoke the Wise One Within (who we will explore more in Chapter 7). Maintaining your loving center and unconditionally embracing all of your parts is an approach embodied by your Wise One Within.

—

1) TUNE BACK IN: REVISIT YOUR GUT CHECK *(5 minutes)*

Let's revisit your Chapter 2 activity, *Part B: Take Inventory of Your Initial Response to Your Parts.*

Note: If there are more parts you have newly identified that you want to describe or explore more in-depth, do that now and add them to your list.

When you did the gut check, did you notice that you had some less than favorable responses to certain parts? Did some feel like old friends?

How did you *feel* toward each part on your list as you identified them?

Though some part of you may be reacting to another part, see if you can connect with your center and embrace the deeper value of each part.

Today, see if you can bring openness and acceptance toward each of these inner aspects, regardless of your initial response. You can do this by being curious about which parts may be reacting to each other, softening resistance that is arising in relation to challenging parts, and trusting that your parts have something valuable to share.

2) BUILDING ON YOUR ILLUSTRATIONS: WHEN PARTS SPEAK (45 minutes)

Next, you can connect with your parts' points of view. In this activity, become curious about what those parts have to offer and *what they want you to know.*

a) First, select two to four parts to work with today. One or two of them can be ones you have affirming feelings toward, and one or two others can be ones that trigger some resistance or judgment.

   If you made visual representations for these parts in Chapter 3, bring those drawings or collages out so you can refer to them for inspiration. If you did not illustrate them yet, you could google an image that might reflect the essence of this part to have a visual aid for this activity.

b) Choose one part to work with at a time, looking at the visual representation you made of them. For each, allow them to share their perspective with you by answering the following prompts from their vantage point (and feel free to create your own!):

› My biggest fear is . . .

› My deepest desire for you is . . .

› My unique strength is . . .

› I want you to know . . .

› A message I have for you today is . . .

c) Using the SoulCollage® Process prompt, write freely, beginning with the sentence stem: *"I Am The One Who . . . "*

Suggestions:

› For all these prompts, you can write out each part's response in a list, in a poem, or in paragraphs.

› As you write, be open to the parts teaching you things about themselves that you did not know you knew. Through letting them speak about who they are and *how* they are, you may learn more about their needs, roles, motivations, desires, and gifts.

› As always, create first and then reflect on what has emerged.

CHAPTER 5 KEY CONCEPTS

› Often, we fixate on the parts of ourselves we see as bright or positive, putting those parts on a pedestal. We may only want to embrace what we determine as good and may try to shun what we deem stormy and bad.

› Just as the sky permits all the weather to express itself in its own way, we, too, can meet our inner storms by making space for difficult feelings or unliked parts.

› Parts themselves are not the problem. What creates friction is how we treat them if we isolate them, neglect them, reject them, or judge them.

› Each part has a role, an identity, a message, and a need.

› It can help to relate to our so-called negative feelings with an understanding that in many cases they are evoked by unmet needs.

› If we are not aware of what needs our parts are trying to meet, we often buy into our habitual strategies reactively, whether they effectively meet our needs or not.

› There might be internal friction when one part is clamoring to be heard. Your parts will reveal their needs to you when you take the time to listen to them and create a welcoming atmosphere for them.

› You can embrace what each part has to say with curiosity and openness to learn from them. When you can accept parts as they are, this allows them to transform naturally because it helps dispel the resistance that keeps things stuck.

›   Rather than forcing yourself to fit a societal norm or even a self-imposed form, connecting with your parts allows for greater authenticity. You can use your understanding of your parts to honor who you really are and rest in that.

›   The goal of this chapter's activity is to allow your parts to communicate with you about their underlying needs, fears, and aspirations so that, through the light and love of your acceptance, your parts can return to their truest essence and form.

CHAPTER 6
THE HIDDEN VALUE IN PROTECTIVE PARTS

Transform Your Inner Critic to Inner Counselor

If you begin to understand what you are without
trying to change it, then what you are
undergoes a transformation.

— J. KRISHNAMURTI

As you saw in Chapter 5, each of your parts has a message, purpose, need, and role in your inner system. In this chapter, we will hone in on the Inner Critic, whose constant criticisms can close the heart, separate you from people you love, and distance you from other parts. You will come to see how the Inner Critic is often trying to keep you safe by using the reliable and predictable strategies of your past. They also may be taking a stand for the standards and values that you or others hold dear.

By acknowledging your Inner Critic's true desires, you can help this part find healthier ways to meet those intentions. As the judgments that formerly blinded them start to soften, this part can become a valuable asset rather than a barrier to your growth. Let's explore how your Inner Critic can transform into an Inner Counselor, a powerful force who finds new ways to bring to life what matters most to you.

WHAT FRIGHTENS YOU IS JUST AFRAID

"You'll never make it."

"Who do you think you are to try that?"

"You'll be squashed by your competition before you even get close."

"You are too much!"

"You are not enough."

"It has already been done so many times. There is no point."

"This has never been done before! There is no proof it will work!"

"Your mom will never forgive you…"

"You will never forgive yourself…"

"Remember what happened *last* time…?"

"Just don't even bother; it's better that way."

Does any of this sound familiar? Since the Inner Critic is often run by fear, they are ready with a million compelling reasons why you should not go for it (whatever your next "it" is). When a part of you is frightened, they can also become the one that most frightens you. In their helplessness, your Inner Critic may become angry or stifling to gain any semblance of power. In their desperation to be heard, they may resort to intimidating you to try to protect you, and thus themself. They are scared that you will be ostracized, harmed, or worse: "fail."

Your nervous Inner Critic wants to control the outcome of a situation that they previously did not feel control over. The Inner Critic can be so harsh because they have seen your hopes or expectations dashed, and they want to prevent history from repeating itself. This part constrains their sense of what is possible based on what they has seen and heard, warning you of difficulties ahead. When a critical part gives you this reality check, it can feel like they are a downer or a naysayer, but they are really trying to offer you a gift.

The Inner Critic's overprotective gestures are often well-intentioned but misguided attempts to connect you to reality. They, too, want to make your aspirations happen, but they are acting within the limitations that they believe reality requires. Keep in mind that the Inner Critic *does* ultimately care about what is important to you, which is precisely the reason that they do not want you to fail at those things.

As you work with the Inner Critic, you might see how they actually want to trust you to succeed—they just need to expand their sense of the many ways for that to happen. Likewise, you can broaden your own perception of the path ahead to include the Inner Critic's most valuable considerations.

THE INNER CRITIC
AS PROTECTOR

Our critical parts believe that they are on guard against imminent danger. Anything unknown, new, and, thus, scary can set them off into an unrelenting rampage of worst-case scenario "what-ifs?" Though the Inner Critic is afraid, they believe they are protecting you. Tragically, they do this by feeding those very fears and berating you with a barrage of "shoulds" and "should nots." They do not yet believe that invaluable lessons and golden opportunities await you on the other side of challenging situations.

Part of why the Inner Critic is hard on you is because they do not distinguish between the different kinds of fear. Some fears are certainly valid as they are designed to signal an urgent danger. Those, we should heed. However, there is often a different kind of fear that actually signals a growth opportunity for you. This fear is stimulated by the fact that you are on the threshold of doing something you have never tried before. This new horizon could be the next level of your performance in sports or arts, speaking in front of a large audience, or entering a challenging conversation with a loved one. The Inner Critic may treat this social fear with the same alarm as the physical fear and urge you to run in the opposite direction.

However, the type of fear that indicates your emerging potential is a clue pointing you toward what will help you grow as a person. You benefit from leaning into those fears so you can move through them, even by simply realizing that they were not what you thought they were. As the expression, often attributed to the famous mythologist Joseph Campbell goes, "The cave you fear to enter holds the treasure you seek."

When you consider something that feels way over your head, your Inner Critic may issue warnings about making such a big leap and may unequivocally push you to deny any invitations to expand. However, when you let your Inner Critic's fear of failing inhibit you from beginning new endeavors at all, then you could end up failing by default. Trying to grow too quickly might feel chaotic and ultimately be unsustainable or provoke an inner backlash. What can be more helpful is to come to your edge and develop your capacity, starting from where you already are.

For example, if public speaking incites panic, perhaps not doing it at all feels comfortable and safe. However, avoiding it keeps you from your goal of sharing your insights with others. On the other hand, trying to overcome that fear by giving a talk to a crowd of 10,000 could likely put your nervous system in a fight or flight response, to say the least. A good middle ground could be taking a public speaking course to practice and then start with smaller talks and build up to larger stages. As you progress through these gradual steps, you will gain more confidence in your abilities. Each time you make it through the next hurdle—one that is challenging but not overwhelming—your Inner Critic will be more assured of your capacity too.

WELCOMING YOUR INNER CRITIC

A common impulse in dealing with the Inner Critic is to silence them as much as possible. The logic behind this is to not let any inner naysaying keep you from your most empowered life. However, one of the costs of rejecting the Inner Critic is that your resistance can create a stronger pushback from this part who is trying desperately to be heard. Just as we learned in Chapter 5, this part is protecting underlying needs that they are trying to meet. As you recognize what they are longing for, you can take a less reactive approach that is not rooted in resistance. You can open space to listen to the Inner Critic, seek to understand them, and gain insight from the valuable messages they seek to bring to your attention.

This approach does not mean that you should indulge your Inner Critic or let them run the show. Yet, it does mean facing them instead of avoiding them or hating them. Their desire for your attention can escalate because your Inner Critic is here for a reason, despite their bad reputation. You cannot squash your Inner Critic (or any of your parts) because they are integral to who you are. Trying to get rid of them is in some ways a denial of an essential piece of what makes you you. Still, these parts may need healing and integration to be updated on how to serve you best.

When the Inner Critic can be heard in their desires and be appreciated, they can express themselves through a grounded authenticity, rather than just trying to do what is "right." When integrated, your Inner Critic can act as your Inner Counselor. They will alert you when you are going too far off the deep end, but they can also help you grow as you forge ahead in a bold yet practical manner.

You can learn to appreciate how the Inner Critic has been trying to support you. Without the Inner Critic, you might float off into your fantasies or abandon yourself in pursuit of unbridled passion. Therefore, rather than reject this part, you can let them voice their concerns and incorporate the most beneficial aspects of what they are aiming to offer.

A PART OF THE WHOLE

Working with the Inner Critic is also about integration with other parts so your whole system can be a team. In addition to their focus on protection, forceful parts (like Inner Critics) may be trying to motivate you. However, since they are initially so stubborn, they may stimulate another part which responds by going off in the other direction, making the schism worse.

Let's suppose your Dreamer amps up their determination to fulfill your desires and gets closer to doing so. In response, your Inner Critic could get just as frantic about keeping you safe in the process. When the Inner Critic pumps the brakes, thinking that your dreams come with too big of a risk or could be a waste of time, then other parts of you could resent them for holding you back.

The Inner Critic can either work with or against other parts, depending on how included they are. Sometimes, the Dreamer gets more rebellious because they feel that the Inner Critic is too strict. In turn, the Inner Critic gets louder precisely because the Dreamer seems to be running wild. As you receive the Inner Critic's valuable feedback more readily, the way they communicate to you and other parts relaxes. In their transformed state, the former critic helps ground your ideals and is not so polarized with other parts.

For example, on an especially bad day at work, your Dreamer may want to submit their resignation letter and hop on the next plane to wherever they can sip a piña colada on a sandy beach. The Dreamer may be taking these drastic measures because they are exacerbated by the Inner Critic, who might be saying, "That is not practical or safe, you have no back-up plan, so you better stay in this job indefinitely!"

On the other hand, you could listen to the Inner Critic, let them become an Inner Counselor, and integrate the advice they give when connected to the bigger picture. In that possible reality, you may decide to create a strategic exit plan for the next year. This would allow you to save up funds and then leave your job on better terms, without burning bridges or throwing caution to the wind.

On the road to your goals, you do not have to speed wildly ahead at 100 miles an hour. Instead, the Inner Counselor can help you buckle your seat belt and go 60, increasing the likelihood of reaching your goals at a steady pace.

YOUR INNER CHAMPION AWAITS

Working with your Inner Counselor can help you be both safe and empowered in your next steps. You do not have to buy into the Inner Critic's old stories or take their methods at face value. The Inner Critic's emotions can feel real, but they are not always grounded in what is *true*. When you listen to them rather than shun them, you can help the Inner Critic see that reality is bigger than what they thought it was. Then, the Inner Critic can come to understand that though its fears may have been both real and partially true in the past, they are not generalizable in every instance. They can see that just because their fear seemed valid or had a purpose at some point does not mean it is the only truth possible now. This shift in how you frame things will allow your Inner Critic to help you ground your aspirations into a viable actuality.

Rather than fearing the Inner Critic by pushing them away, you can trust that you are whole enough and steady enough to handle lovingly what they are trying to offer. Thus, you can be open to them with curiosity, so they feel understood in their viewpoint. When you do that, they will often feel freer to release the unhealthy strategies formed in the past, recognizing that their pressuring stance does not actually serve you.

One of Richard Schwartz's great realizations with Internal Family Systems was that parts could take on new roles and qualities. Like with the other parts we have seen, the Inner Critic can reveal their true nature and soften the way they relate to you. We saw this in Chapter 4, when Ayden dialogued with his Inner Critic and his Muse about shaping his future career path. When the Inner Critic was honored for his emphasis on structure yet freed from the pressure and stress of rushing, he then shifted into becoming the Inner Architect of Ayden's journey toward more meaningful work. In his new position, Ayden's former Inner Critic continued to keep him grounded in reality but also collaborated with his other parts to help move Ayden toward what was important to him.

GUARDS AND GUARDIANS

One way to think of the Inner Critic's ability to shift is to consider the archetypes of a Guard and a Guardian. These roles appear so similar yet are so different. The energy of a guard is one that is protective.

Yet, they lose sleep, wearily not allowing their eyes to close for fear of attack. A guard is armed and armored, defensively gripping their sword as tightly as their shield. A guard is fierce, alert, and refuses to rest. They make no excuses and takes none as well.

On the other hand, a Guardian has the same job—to protect and oversee—but does so with more compassion and care. Like Gandalf from Lord of the Rings, a Guardian is strong but not unyielding. Their nurturing energy protects by connecting with what is going on within and around them. They flow in relation to the whole interplay of things. Unlike the suspicious guard, the Guardian trusts in something greater and moves from that place. Guardians are wise, quiet, and graceful in their duty of leading. A Guardian acts swiftly when needed but remains centered even in the somberness of their responsibilities.

Your Inner Critic can shift from being like a guard to acting as a guardian. As you work with your own wary Inner Critic, you will be able to shift from being overly alert and suspicious, almost like an overprotective parent yelling "CAREFUL!" around every corner. Instead, your acknowledgment of the Inner Critic's value invites this figure to become grounded in their actions. Thus, as your new Counselor, Advisor, Champion, or Guardian, this part can now engage in behaviors that are *full of care.*

When they are running the show unattended, the Inner Critic can become a barrier to your goals. However, when they are more integrated, they can become a grounding force that bridges reality and your dreams. What the Inner Critic needs most is to learn to trust—in the world around them, in your capacity to meet your circumstances, and in the other parts of you. Working to cultivate trust within helps you to marshal *all* parts of yourself forward, despite the initial fear that your Inner Critic might have experienced. To cultivate this trust, we must acknowledge the Inner Critic's perspective and not override their concerns.

When you get your Inner Critic on board, they will no longer halt your progress out of fear of the unfamiliar. Instead, the Inner Critic becomes an ally in moving wisely into the next phase of your development. Thus, what formerly stimulated intimidation inside of you can now inspire your strength and evoke an ability to meet your circumstances with grace.

—

Now, let's see how Grace navigated her relationship with her Inner Critic. Grace initially felt that her Inner Critic's outdated notions of perfection held her back from moving toward a free expression and pursuit of her aspirations. In speaking with her Inner Critic through guided visualization, she allowed her to share her true intentions, thereby gaining a new relationship with this part.

GRACE'S SELF-LOVE JOURNEY: MEETING THE CRITIC WHO CARED

Grace had just turned 28 years old and was eager to get her budding social media marketing company off the ground. She loved this line of work and wanted to be able to turn this passion into a full-time endeavor. However, Grace also felt stunted by feelings of self-doubt, not trusting that she was capable of having her business be anything but a side pursuit. She also felt pressure from her mother, who was not very encouraging of her taking the risk to transition from traditional employment.

Every time Grace would sit down to work on her new business, her Inner Critic popped up and warned her—not so gently—about the frightening possibility of letting herself (and her family) down. The contrast between this antagonizing inner voice and Grace's desires caused an inner tension.

Grace admitted feeling stuck regarding her next steps, saying, "I want to have certainty with my new direction, so I put everything on hold because I don't want it to be less than perfect!" This tension caused Grace to feel like she was drifting through life in ambiguity.

In our session together, Grace began by closing her eyes and settling into a peaceful scene in her mind's eye. Then, we invited her Inner Critic to join her there.

Grace: She has arrived, and I am not happy to see her. This is interesting! My Critic—who is so afraid of failing—looks like the supposed "perfect" version of me. This part is still me, but a younger version of me—like when I was in college and obsessed about my body, caring so much about my physique. She is the fittest and skinniest I have ever been but has a look of so much panic on her face. She is miserable! She has frantic energy, darting eyes, and all sorts of frown lines. This all just popped up automatically! Wow.

Though Grace was surprised by how immediately she conjured this image of her Inner Critic, she felt it was aptly aligned with her internal experience of striving to color within the perceived lines of socially acceptable choices. As Grace encountered this polished and flawless version of herself, she described feeling a weight inside her chest that was being pulled down by the Inner Critic's presence.

Grace: My gut response to this college self is that I am surprised and annoyed, like, "What is *she* doing here? She is not going to ruin this meditation for me!" Her presence here already takes away from the sense of serenity and expansiveness I was feeling before. Suddenly even my surroundings feel smaller.

To work with this critical part (nicknamed "Gray"), I asked Grace to speak to her directly. Grace began to share her side of the story with her Inner Critic.

Grace: I feel like there is so much that I am capable of and that I want to explore, experience, and learn. But I feel that I don't have the chance because you sabotage every adventure. It is like you possess me, and suddenly, I feel my heart beating fast, and I lose my words, and my thoughts run at a thousand miles an hour. I am unable to continue because you plant so much doubt in my head! Whenever I take a step forward and feel I am growing in my sense of self-worth, hope, and courage, you let me go for a little bit—just to give me a taste. Then, you pop up and remind me maybe there's something wrong with me, that I do not have what it takes, and that I am selfish. It is like you know what buttons to push that render me paralyzed. It is frustrating because I have never gone down a road long enough to clarify what I really think about it—because you won't let me. You keep showing up uninvited, and you try to manipulate me. Now, I do not know where to go anymore because you are always going to be there. This has to stop because it is not helping. Plus, you must be tired too after years of doing this—it is time to talk about it.

I repeated these words back to Grace so she could hear what she had just said to Gray. Then, I asked her to check in with how Gray was feeling in response to receiving those words.

Grace: Gray feels frowny, focused, and intent on explaining to me why I am wrong. She's determined to share that how she sees things is the way it is.

Now, it was Gray's turn to speak. Grace did her best to empathize with her Inner Critic and now began speaking from Gray's vantage point.

Gray: You think I like doing this? I don't enjoy badgering you, but I feel like I have to because you won't take any action otherwise. I feel like I have been good to you for all these years. I have been looking out for you. Maybe it is inconvenient, or you lose a little bit of sleep, but I have saved you from your crazy ideas. All I am trying to do is protect you from pain that you can't handle. You have been hurt before. You like to take risks, and I admire that about you, but how will you make your dreams come true? You expect things to work out easily, and when the going gets tough, you just give up! That tendency to quit tells me that if things get really hard, you'll want to be coddled and taken care of, like when you were a kid. As you get older, and if you start your own company, you will be on your own! Even if I have to be the contrarian naysayer at times, that's my role. I am really just trying to protect you because I want what is best for you.

Here, we paused for Grace to take a few deep breaths, hear those words reflected back, and tune in to how she felt hearing Gray's side of the story.

Grace: I actually feel very understood and seen. There is ease now. Also, I realize that there is truth to this, but it is not the whole truth; it is just part of it. As I listened to my Inner Critic, I started to see that this person is a lot like my mom. I can see how her worry—like the part of my mom when she gets judgmental and critiques me—is actually coming from a loving place. I have always perceived that approach as mean and overbearing, but now I can see how it is derived from love.

I asked if Grace could extend gratitude to Gray for the intention of protecting her. Grace agreed and affirmed tearfully, "We've forged a huge step forward for us."

As we came out of the meditation and debriefed, Grace commented, "Wow, I can only breathe through my mouth because my nose is plugged from crying! That was so cathartic. I feel relief, freedom, and fluidity. Rather than feeling stagnant like a well, I feel the sense of a soothing river. It is not a gushing river, but there is the peaceful white noise of a river in the distance. It felt really good to face the thing I was so afraid of and put it all into words, especially recognizing there is truth in both. I see now that the fear I have had from my past is not unreasonable and that the point is not to get rid of Gray, but to work on our relationship so that her fear is not my default mode."

After this encounter with Gray, Grace gained more momentum to work on her business without stalling or feeling guilty. She began to be open to being curious about her Inner Critic rather than at war with her. Even just connecting to the intentions, needs, and messages of your Inner Critic can help you to begin to transform your relationship with them and loosen their grip on your life.

Sometimes, as with Grace's Inner Critic, the warnings, nagging doubts, or perceived limitations that they bombard us with could be messages that we have internalized from our worried parents, demanding teachers, teasing peers or other societal influences. When our Inner Critics believe these skeptical and scathing words to be reality, we can feel undermined by such judgments.

The Inner Critic's drive to have you do better and be better often stems from their fear of abandonment. They may have taken other's judgements to heart and created strict rules for what they deem is acceptable behavior. In some ways, the Inner Critic could be seen as our false self, the one we present to others that might not be authentic but is bending over backward to earn belonging.

Thus, to keep you connected and safe, the Inner Critic usually wants to obey the rules they believe are necessary. However, when they get to communicate and be heard, your whole system can connect to a more accurate understanding that incorporates your current abilities and possibilities. You can then determine supportive guidelines and good practices that are not just dictated by old stories, society, or other people, but rather by the wise counsel of your inner team.

—

In our next example, we will explore how to transform the Inner Critic into an ally instead of a perceived enemy through recognizing the gifts they are attempting to give.

DARIA'S STORY:
THE TEACHER LEARNS A LESSON

Daria was coming up on her annual review at work. She was nervous about feedback from her boss and had doubts about whether she would be given a promotion.

When Daria met her Inner Critic through a guided visualization, the image of a teacher came to her immediately. This Teacher part was prim and proper, wearing cat eyeglasses and clutching a ruler in her hand. Daria described the Teacher as standing up stiffly, with arms and legs apart, gripping her ruler really tightly and squinting her eyes angrily.

Daria commented that it made sense that her Critic appeared as a teacher since Daria had often felt dominated by authority figures such as professors or previous bosses. "I never felt like I had mentorship where those a step ahead of me were eager to see me grow," she stated sadly. In the Teacher's presence, Daria judged herself as "less than."

To Daria's surprise, she noticed that the Teacher was accompanied by another part—a shorter hip-height version of Daria dressed in frayed dark garb. This other part appeared dull and disheveled, with dark circles under her eyes and no luminosity to her face. Daria felt very sorry for this weary version of her, whom she named the "Lost One."

The Lost One was scared of the Teacher, resigning herself to being beaten down. The Lost One was exhausted and despondent but felt tied to the Teacher. In this inner scene, the Teacher was off in a corner, not making eye contact.

As we engaged with these parts, we approached the Teacher and asked why she was so mean to the Lost One.

Teacher: Because I have a lot of RAGE, and it feels good to dominate over someone.

Daria: That is not nice, though. That is a horrible thing to do to someone else!

Teacher: That is how I know how to communicate.

Daria: *(laughs to herself)* Well, maybe you should get another communication method!

The Teacher did not like this response, nor find it funny. Daria got curious about her Critic.

Daria: Why are you doing this? What do you want? What are you afraid of?

Teacher: I want to feel in control. When I see the Lost One, that is my nightmare, so I bully her. I keep her at a distance, so that way I will never be like her—but inside I feel like the Lost One.

Daria was struck by this insight that the Teacher was acting so harshly because she saw a part of herself in the Lost One. She realized that the Teacher was trying to push that aspect of Daria's system away to keep Daria (and thus herself) from that sorry fate.

Daria: *(commenting)* The Teacher is super defensive for no reason! I guess she doesn't want to lose her spot, her place.

Jeanine to Teacher: What is the threat? What are you afraid of losing?

Teacher: I am afraid of failure, and to prevent that, I am exerting power over other people, which makes me feel better about my situation.

Daria: *(commenting)* The Teacher actually feels really lonely. She sees that her approach is not working, and she feels tired too. She may look very strong, but she's really sad inside.

Daria now felt a wave of compassion for the Teacher and reached out her hand to touch her elbow. The Teacher remained stiff but accepted Daria's gesture, though she would not go for a handshake or a hug.

Daria: Thank you for contributing to my ambition and my drive— though I think you go overboard.

Teacher: Well, I don't know how to ease up.

Jeanine: Would you, if you could?

Teacher: That is a hard question. Not right away, but I can start to loosen the reins to a certain extent.

Daria told the Teacher that she understood and was grateful for her help so far, then reached to give her a hug.

Teacher: *(teary-eyed)* I thought nobody liked me, thank you. It is hard to receive because I always give, give, give.

The Lost One was wary of getting close but was beginning to find her voice.

The Lost One: You have always beaten me down; I can't trust you. You say this now, but is it really going to change?" *(still, she ventured a bit closer)*

Teacher: I can't promise it will change 100% overnight, but I can make progress gradually.

The Lost One: Okay, I can accept progress. And if you can listen to what I have to say, we can make something work.

They shook hands in a formal manner, as if sealing a business transaction. Daria noticed that the Teacher ultimately did want to help and be a positive influence.

Daria: *(commenting)* She knows she bludgeons me with ambition and demands perfection, but now she knows that her approach is not working. I don't want her to change completely, but to lessen her degree of pressure.

Jeanine: If your Wise One Within could enter now and give this Teacher a gift, what would it be?

Daria: It's very metaphorical! It's a diamond and a chisel. It's like she is trying to convey, "You are chiseling the diamond of your gifts down to nothing by overdoing it. Make sure when you look at this beautiful diamond, you realize it's perfect just as it is, and don't chisel it."

Daria: *(reflecting)* Wow, I see now that I've been doing that to myself for a very long time—constantly putting pressure on myself and not taking things day by day. I didn't realize how much I am hurting myself in doing this.

As the Teacher received the gifts, she started to cry. The Teacher did not know she was doing harm; she had thought she was helping.

Teacher: *(starts sobbing)* I am so sorry! I want to help the Lost One and give her a break so she can sleep. Now I know that underneath her rags, there is a beautiful woman just waiting to come out. I thought the Lost One was just lazy and coasting. I didn't realize that she was so timid because I was bludgeoning her so much.

Daria and the Teacher formed a pact to be kinder to each other with this new understanding.

Jeanine: Who would the Teacher be in a healthy new role?

Daria: She would be like a Guru! Like a life teacher, not a structured teacher who is rigid and uptight about rules. I think she would support me to go where my heart flows and do what brings me joy.

Jeanine: Does the Teacher like that idea?

Daria: Yes and No. On the one hand, she thinks that is great, but she doesn't want me to waste time going with the flow all the time.

Jeanine: What does that look like as a middle ground?

Daria: She says she wants to be more like my late grandmother. My Nana had profound words and a lot of wisdom for me. When I was stressed, she would calm me down and always know what to say, though she wouldn't mince words. She would help me get organized too since she was very grounded and practical.

The Teacher thus felt best taking on a similar role as Nana, as the Encourager. In this new form, the Encourager could help Daria feel more faith in herself, her work, and her future. As she continued to advance in her career, Daria could rely on the Encourager to ensure a high quality of work. She began to feel increasingly confident in her abilities and more prepared for her annual review, both inside and out.

As you can see from Daria's story, these parts are malleable and have their own emotions. When we work with our critical parts and make space to listen to them, we do not have to agree with them nor force them to change. Rather, we commit to seeing where we have become shrouded by counterproductive protective mechanisms and give our critics an opportunity to support us more effectively. In meeting the truth of who they are, we remember who we have always been.

CHAPTER 6 ACTIVITY:

Being Curious about
Your Inner Critic

JOURNAL PROMPTS: FROM GUARD TO GUARDIAN *(1 hour)*

› Take some time to answer at least three of the questions in each category below.

› Choose ones that speak to you and also ones that bring up resistance (because maybe there is something valuable to find on the other side of what you are seeking to avoid).

› After you write out your responses to these questions, reflect on your new relationship with your Inner Critic. What are you still curious about? How can you apply your learnings to a challenge in your life today?

Inner Critic as Guard:

› Where, or in what circumstances, do you feel most critical of others?

› Does your judgment of others resemble your judgment of yourself?

› In what areas are you hardest on yourself?

› How does it make you feel when you are self-critical?

› Do any other parts of you rebel against self-criticism? What are these like? What do they need?

› What might your Inner Critic be trying to protect you from or avoid happening?

> Can you appreciate your Inner Critic for their efforts to keep you safe?

> What other noble intentions does the Inner Critic have for you?

Inner Counselor as Guardian:

> If your Inner Critic stepped into their role as a Counselor or Guardian, what would change?

> How can your Inner Critic continue to serve your inner system in a healthier way?

> What would your Inner Critic like to be called when they shift from issuing fear-based judgements to supporting you with care?

> How can you appreciate the transformation of this part?

> What will you do to keep in touch with this transformed part and reaffirm that they belong?

> How can your transformed part bring their new wisdom to a challenging situation in your life?

CHAPTER 6 KEY CONCEPTS

› Your fear to venture forth can stem from your Inner Critic's warnings about perceived future loss, based on past experiences.

› Some fears give valid warnings, but others signal that you are on the precipice of a valuable new developmental step. Your Inner Critic does not necessarily distinguish between those two fears when you face something new.

› In many cases, the Inner Critic formed to help protect you. They do so in the only way they know how—through judgment, fear, and worry.

› Your Inner Critic is often the embodiment of your perception of someone who is uncompromising in their quest for perfection. For example, they might show up as an overbearing teacher, a strict nun, a guard, a courtroom judge, or even the most "polished" version of you.

› The Inner Critic may not be up to date with the actual possibilities in your life because they rely on past pains or difficulties to anticipate the threats ahead.

› The Inner Critic may have a limited conception of reality, but ultimately is trying to connect you to the truth, so you can be safe from harm.

› The strategies the Inner Critic uses to achieve their aims may be outdated or unskillful. They need to trust that other parts are holding these same needs for security and realism, so that they can relax.

› When you get clarity about what your Inner Critic cares about, honoring those needs can shift their approach.

› When you encounter an Inner Critic acting as your inner guard and trying to protect you in a defensive or alarmist way, you can listen to their messages rather than seek to banish them. They may then shift from acting like a weary and wary guard to a calm and soothing Guardian.

› By exploring your relationship with this protective part, you may see that they become a useful ally, aide, overseer, or advisor who can bring in a much-needed perspective.

III.

TRUSTING YOUR INNER COMPASS

So far, you have met many of your parts and worked with them to connect with their messages and gifts.

With the tools in this final section, you can allow the authentic fullness of who you are to inform your next steps. With your Wise One Within at the helm, you can bring all your parts aboard in the direction of your dreams.

In committing to integration and wholeness, you will feel more at home within your own being. What is more, you can lead your life with increased love, grace, connection, and clarity.

CHAPTER 7
YOUR WISE ONE WITHIN

Connect with Your Deeper Truth for Guidance

Ego says, "Once everything falls into place, I'll feel peace."
Spirit says, "Find your peace, and then
everything will fall into place."

— MARIANNE WILLIAMSON

We house supportive resources deep within ourselves that are available when we are ready to access them. Admittedly, these may be harder to reach when many noisy voices cloud our inner space. By now, we have had a chance to work with the parts most hungry for our attention. We have learned to acknowledge the loud ones' cries and to lean in to hear the softer voices as well. Since we have allowed these parts to get their needs met and start harmonizing with each other, more room can open now in our minds and hearts. In this calmer atmosphere, we can more easily access a presence that has been awaiting the opportunity to share itself: your Wise One Within.

Just as the steady earth offers a foundation underfoot even when we take it for granted, the presence of the Wise One Within dwells as a reliable undercurrent to our aliveness. Though we may not always be aware or receptive to their energy, the Wise One Within is an ever-ready companion who is the gateway to our innermost knowing.

The Wise One Within is a benevolent and unconditionally loving figure who maintains a generous, grounded, and composed presence. As the personification of your inner resources, this wisdom keeper helps to unite all the events and emotions in your life with a graceful embrace. Reverent and sovereign, the Wise One Within holds the strength, courage, and fortitude to meet your life's circumstances and help you through them.

Your Wise One Within houses a wellspring of deep inner truth. In an old story, a man is sitting on a box every day, begging for coins. He feels desperate, lonely, and hopeless. One day, a sage comes along and asks him what he is sitting on.

As the man looks underneath him, he finds he had been seated on a treasure chest the whole time! Likewise, we can all contact our own golden nature if we shift our perspective inward for the beauty and riches we may overlook or take for granted.

The concepts and tools in this chapter will help you connect to your inner resources in a way that resonates with you. Through encountering the reassuring presence of your Wise One Within, you can begin to settle into serenity, feeling increasingly sure of your choices because they come from an aligned place inside you.

Whether you imagine this wise being as an aspect of your own self or as an external mentor, it can be a doorway into cultivating a more consistent state of well-being. This grand and humble archetype can help you to feel connected, loved, and loving—from the inside out. Learning to lean on your Wise One Within's intuition can help you develop more meaning in your days, generate greater ease, and increase a sense of depth and freedom in your life.

Your Wise One Within can help you live from your center, having faith in who you are. Let's explore who this Wise One Within is and how you can evoke and trust their presence.

QUALITIES OF YOUR
WISE ONE WITHIN

Alternatively referred to as the Self, or the Higher Self, this element of parts work brings a loving witness to your personal exploration. The Wise One Within is not a part so much as a container that is expansive enough to hold all the other parts' emotions and energy. The Wise One Within can help heal other parts with the natural acceptance that they bring. In some guided visualizations, the Wise One Within can be called upon to preside over or even mediate the interactions with other parts because their presence can create harmony rather than fear or judgment. When you welcome other parts into your mental field, bringing in your Wise One Within adds an essential sense of perspective. Connecting with your Wise One Within can help you meet any of your parts with love, helping to direct and protect your system as you dive deeper.

In prior chapters, you have learned how to relate with your parts, witness them non-judgmentally, and approach them with a welcoming state of mind. Fostering this loving acceptance of your parts has already evoked qualities of your Wise One Within, who is precisely the embodiment of that kind of space. By embracing each of your parts' messages, you have begun to unify their strategies according to the deeper needs that they share.

As we discussed in Chapter 5, when seeking to observe ourselves, we can benefit by adopting a vantage point that is like the sky for all our internal weather. Whereas the parts play out a lot of the weather of your inner world, the trustworthy Wise One Within remains steady and spacious as the sky. Tom Holmes, author of *Parts Work*, describes the Self in his book, "One person has said that it is like water: it is clear, and quiet, and calm, and doesn't have a 'personality' like the often colorful parts of the inner system do." Though the Wise One Within occurs differently to everyone, it can help to think of this figure as a space, the keeper of your truest and deepest nature, who tends to every encounter with a nurturing attention.

As the seat of infinite love and unwavering compassion, the Wise One Within can be a beacon of light, allowing all of your parts to be held and understood without making any of them "wrong" or "bad." The encounter between what feels broken and what feels whole may be where healing happens. The Wise One Within's gentle acceptance reminds us that instead of feeling like we are continually missing the mark in our quest for perfection, we can work with what we have. When we rely on our inner resources, like the ones revealed to us by the Wise One Within, we may find that we have much more than we anticipated. Even though we always see with our own eyes, we can change where we see from—and thus what we see—by shifting our perspective.

With the gentle and uplifting care of the Wise One Within, our inner worlds can thus undergo a transformation akin to kintsugi, the Japanese art of pottery repair where the cracks of broken pots are filled with gold. This process makes the once useless pot now even more unique and valuable. Likewise, when tended to with the reparative ability of loving attention, our most tender places can also become the seat of our greatest gifts and offerings. Instead of living from our perceived brokenness, we can tap into the wise aspect of our being which helps make sense of all the pieces.

CONNECTING WITH
YOUR INNER COMPASS

As a doorway connecting the self beyond itself, there can often be a spiritual tone to the work with the Wise One Within. This figure could be likened to the inner representative of your soul, a personified aspect of spirit who may be any gender or genderless. Parts work is both personal and universal and can be accessed with the spiritual language you already have. I have worked with people who hold various spiritual and secular views (religious, philosophical, and faith traditions; spiritual without affiliation; agnostic; and atheist). Each person has had a unique interpretation of the characteristics of their Wise One Within. Yet, most of the people I have worked with have also shared a common sense of serenity and comfort when connecting with this element of themselves.

This compassionate aspect of oneself (or way of being *with* oneself) grants a perspective similar to a meditative state. Your peaceful Wise One Within meets each moment as it is. Meditation and mindfulness are both gateways into relating to the Wise One Within, and they are also states that can result from connecting with this energy. Whereas meditation is a practice, your connection with the Wise One Within is a *relationship*. Meditation evokes awareness, creates openness, and is space itself. The Wise One Within has all these qualities but also engages the faculty of the imagination and uses symbolism to be understood. You can see this relationship with your Wise One Within as a creative and vivid doorway into your own knowing and peace. By tuning in to the Wise One Within's presence, you can learn to cultivate equanimity, a state of calm and inner stability, especially when under pressure or surrounded by chaos—real or perceived.

Connecting with your Wise One Within is not an all-or-nothing experience. It can happen in gradations, and even the intention to connect is a meaningful starting point. There are also many paths and possible modalities for accessing this source of inner wisdom. For some, connecting with the Wise One Within through imagery and visualization may come easily and may be very supportive. Others may find the gateway to their inner knowing through meditation, journaling, art, or creative movement. Each person may even find different access points to this way of being at different points in their lives. You can try different avenues of cultivating a relationship with your Wise One Within from any state. As you do so, maintain an approach of curiosity and openness toward accessing your inner gifts, allowing them to evolve as you explore further.

If you find it difficult to imagine a personal embodiment of your own inner Wise One Within, it can be helpful to imagine a familiar source of comfort outside of yourself. This person could be a real-life mentor or a famous figure who inspires you and whom you aspire to emulate. It could be someone in history (e.g., Mother Theresa or Gandhi). Or, you might imagine a mythical/mythological character who is at once humble, noble, and majestic (akin to your own inner Dumbledore from Harry Potter, or an elven queen such as Galadriel from Lord of the Rings). Those who have a specific faith may choose to invoke the presence of one of their enlightened teachers for guidance, support, and comfort. For some, the Wise One Within appears as a light, a color, a feeling, a sensation in the body, or a presence.

My client Ebonie saw her Wise One Within emerge as an older woman with curly white hair who appeared with a warm smile. Ebonie said her Wise One Within was "absolutely comfortable in herself—despite what others might think." Ebonie described this figure as "almost like that Grandmother Willow tree from the Pocahontas movie, but in human form. She wears a dress like a nightgown made with floral fabric. It has got lively colors and patterns, like something my grandma would wear." Ebonie mentioned that people would not consider her Wise One Within conventionally pretty but that her kind features made her beautiful. When she pictured her Wise One Within, Ebonie described her as full of ease, unhurried, and possessing a strong willingness to offer companionship to Ebonie. "It fills me with delight," Ebonie shared. She explained, "It feels like seeing someone for the first time and also feeling like you already know them, even though we've never met."

Encountering your Wise One Within as an external figure like Ebonie did here allows you to build a relationship with this wise being more easily. In whichever way this inner guide is represented to you, you will be able to feel the truth of the Wise One Within as its interactions evoke an inner nod or feeling of relief.

The Wise One Within's actions, presence, and messages will always reassure, resonating on a level of pure knowing. If you sense something that feels funny or off, you may have another part that you are confusing with the Wise One Within. In that case, you can ask them to step aside and identify who they are, if possible. Then, continue to engage the Wise One Within who creates a sense of deep rest in you.

YOUR WISE ONE IS ALREADY ALWAYS YOU

The Wise One Within is not an ideal self you should aspire to be like. Rather, it is a divine spark within you that you can embody more and more. Some people put their Higher Self on a pedestal where they idealize, romanticize, or are even jealous of this aspect. However, your Wise One Within is not just an imagined "future self," but rather an "already always" place within you. In other words, this element of your nature is pristine, infinite, and ever-present—it has always been and will always be. The wholeness, dignity, and sovereignty of your being is already there, so there is nowhere to get to and no one to become.

You might sometimes be tempted to visualize the Wise One Within as your future self, but these personas are slightly different. Your image of your future self could be a projection of your current feelings, fears, or hopes for the path ahead. Some people see imagery of their future selves that scares them, such as a darkened or haggard figure that feels ominous or disappointing. Others might see their future self as someone who has resolved the challenges they are currently facing. Fast-forwarding through time might grant perspective and relief from any preoccupation that will eventually become a non-issue. Connecting with an image of a more mature version of you certainly can be interesting and give a good message about where you think you are headed, even inviting you to re-examine your current path.

However, encountering the Wise One Within will be different since it is not bound by time or circumstance. Since the Wise One Within represents the core essence of who you are throughout time and even beyond it, it will always offer you comfort. The Wise One Within may not even look like you, yet you will feel steadied by the loving composure it brings. You can inhabit this way of being whenever you reach out to call upon its presence.

HUMAN AND DIVINE

Connecting with your Wise One Within can often evoke the recognition of your own wholeness. This space within you might feel like experiencing a moment of grace that transcends the norms of everyday life and lets you know you are held. In terms of energy, your Wise One Within can be interpreted as the meeting place of what is human and what is divine. As the Serbian proverb goes, "Be humble for you are made of earth. Be noble for you are made of stars."

Like a drop in the ocean, each of us is singular in form while also containing the vastness of a shared essence. Inhabiting the presence of your Wise One Within helps you connect with that essential core of yourself in more areas of your life. Still, it is important not to turn your relationship with your Wise One Within into a quest for perfection. Even as we aspire toward more noble ways of being, we will always continue to contend with our own vulnerabilities and challenges. Tom Holmes makes a key distinction about the Wise One Within, which Internal Family Systems calls the Self:

> There is a danger that we may get the idea that we should somehow find ourselves in a constant state of peace, of calm, of Self. Given human nature, none of us will constantly be living in a state of Self. The reality is that most of the time our consciousness bounces around from parts to the Self, from less aware to more aware and back again, but the Self can become increasingly available as we exercise our awareness.

LISTENING WITHIN

Connecting to our Wise One Within helps us to recognize and actualize our gifts. By touching base with our Wise One Within, we can gain simple yet profound guidance on the path towards our life's aspirations. We begin to feel aligned with the energy of what we want to move toward, even if it is not visibly here yet. Though, of course, action is necessary to propel our aims forward, aligned action must first begin with *listening*.

By listening to our inner wisdom, we learn to let go, let be, and let *in*. If we look deeper, we will find that we already know our own answers. Therefore, it is a matter of being curious, asking the right questions, and being open to receiving a response. We find direction by tuning into where we are and being open to taking the right next step. If we tap into the deep wisdom housed in our intuition and communicated through our bodies, we can find clarity and peace as we move in both our inner and outer worlds.

Now, we will witness the power of opening to the guidance of the Wise One Within through the stories of Rose and Carole. In these examples, both women listen to the messages of their Wise Ones Within to find greater self-acceptance through the process of guided visualization.

ROSE'S ENCOUNTER WITH
HER WISE ONE WITHIN

When Rose met me, she was looking for clarity on how to show up authentically in her life. She was feeling split between her personal and professional roles. Spirituality was a core focus in her life and she was exploring how to facilitate healing work with different modalities, such as Reiki. However, in her serious government job, she worried that she could not bring that integral side of herself to work. Since she spent so much time in the office, she felt she was compartmentalizing aspects of her identity.

In our guided meditation sessions, she discovered that she had a Wise One Within that presented itself viscerally through feelings and sensations instead of as a personification. Rose described that, "She seems less like a figure coming toward me, and more like a white lilac-blue light that comes behind my eyes. It is like a light that I feel inside, rather than one that shines on me."

As soon as she encountered this quality of being, tears sprung to Rose's eyes. She said she was sad at being estranged from this presence and was missing the feeling of unconditional love that emanated from her connection to it.

As she checked back in with this wise being, Rose described, "Now, I feel her acknowledging the conversation we are having and the color of her light is deepening to a darker blue of peacock. She communicates through color and energy rather than words or action."

Rose then described a second wave of sadness, thinking herself unde-serving of this interaction because she felt she had neglected her Wise One Within for so long. Rose said she had let herself become trapped in feeling small, in contrast to the magnanimity which she felt in the energy of the wise presence.

Connecting further with her Wise One Within, Rose said, "I think there is this sense from her that *I am* this bigger energy, and that I have always been this. It feels like it is just about returning to this aspect of myself."

As she was feeling this, her Wise One Within's energy reassured her, "Yes, this is really you. Remember . . . " Rose felt sad that she had lost touch with the Wise One Within. Yet, as they were connecting, Rose felt no judgment from her guide, but rather a warm glowing feeling.

Rose described, "Now, I am worried that the way I feel her is too subtle. It takes a while to reach her, and I am concerned that it won't be easy to access each time."

I wondered if Rose feared that she would not be able to access this feeling as easily in the future. So I asked Rose about her underlying desire and need in the moment, to which Rose replied, "I want her to be more present."

I suggested she could request that of the Wise One Within. Rose, then, with shivering tears, asked the presence, "Can you reach me? Can you stay?"

The color behind her eyes got clearer as she felt a sense of a resounding "YES," and then the color came even a bit closer.

Rose continued, "I want to ask, '*how* can you reach me?' The color is really subtle to connect with, but I love color." Rose loved to paint and mentioned that the color she was seeing in this presence was her favorite one.

Rose reported back, "She is saying, 'The connection happens when you meditate or do your healing work.' Oh, and I feel something happening in my hands. My hands are what I use to do healing or painting, so they might be a doorway. It feels like when I do activities with my hands, that is another way for her to communicate in addition to appearing as this colored light."

In closing, Rose chose to say goodbye and thank the Wise One Within, and, in doing so, she received a knowing sense that she could trust this new bond. She affirmed, "I now know that I can connect whenever I wish and there is no need to try to cling to this experience to take it with me." Rose committed to keep following these breadcrumbs placed by the Wise One Within as pathways to connection with her light.

As you can see in Rose's story, no matter in what shape or form it shows up, the presence of the Wise One Within can help to soothe your inner system and encourage a feeling of home and belonging, right where you are.

—

In our next example, Carole had done some work with parts like you have done so far in this book. She had enjoyed the process of getting to know them, but she had not yet met her Wise One Within. As she made this connection, she was more able to center herself in her own sense of worth rather than seeking outside approval.

CAROLE'S STORY: MEETING THE WISE ONE WITHIN

Carole was a self-proclaimed workaholic at a software engineering firm, and she wanted support with work-life balance and confidence. She was feeling lost and "not good enough." She told me, "I'm almost sixty! It is time for me to learn to love myself and not compare myself to everyone else." To cope with the intense stress of her childhood, Carole had aimed to perform and succeed in an attempt to earn love in an environment where she did not feel nurtured. As an adult, she had been deriving self-worth from her job for years until she realized that this approach was not satisfying her, and she wanted trust and acceptance to come from within.

Carole shared, "I want to recover the joy that I haven't felt in ages. I can't remember the last time I felt joy. I tell my staff, 'We can enjoy the journey,' but I cannot seem to live that philosophy in my own life."

Here, I pointed out the distinction between knowledge and knowing. Carole understood the concept of self-acceptance mentally. However, information is not the same as transformation. While we may know something intellectually, it does not necessarily cause a shift in us until that awareness becomes a knowing that includes the mind and also the heart. When we experience something viscerally on many levels, we cannot unknow it because we have lived it. Thus, the parts work with Carole would use visualization to help her to know joy and self-love experientially.

In prior sessions, Carole had already encountered some of her cynical parts, getting to see how they popped up when she was hard on herself. Carole felt these jaded parts were loud and at the fore, but she was learning to pay attention to their messages. When she was ready and curious to meet her Wise One Within, we began the inner deep dive through some guided visualization.

As Carole felt more relaxed and open, I introduced her to the Wise One Within, asking her to describe what was coming up for her as she envisioned this being.

As she imagined her guide, Carole said, "I am not big on describing, but I feel that this person coming towards me is amazing! So prominent and calm. I just feel good that she's looking at me. She's looking at me—and I think she is proud of me!"

We paused to let that feeling wash over her before Carole continued to share what the Wise One Within was communicating.

Carole: She tells me that she is keeping an eye on me, is watching me and will be there with me. That's how I feel that this is . . . It's just . . . It is okay! She's *affirming* me.

Jeanine: How does it feel?

Carole: It is emotional. I am tearing up. I feel so connected. We are not hugging; that's not what I need. I needed that nod of, "I am proud of you. You're doing good, and I am here with you. You're not alone."

Jeanine: You are supported. You are held.

Carole: I have never felt this before. I have never felt that somebody has been so proud of me—and to realize that it is myself is such a relief!

Jeanine: This is always available, has been, and will be . . .

Carole: *(still in tears)* I've never met her before. I don't know what she looks like. I just get an essence with the feeling—not a face or name—but a real feeling of a presence there that brings me to a feeling of home.

After we wrapped up the encounter with her Wise One Within, Carole reflected on the experience, telling me, "I've heard many times, 'Love yourself and give yourself a hug,' but I never knew how to connect to that. This felt real and now I know it more fully. I am going to do that again!"

For Carole, after a few sessions, she was able to admit, "I work for a company that has no heart and is callous, but now I have something new. I have a belief that I am good and that I can be good at what I do.

I can know that while also remembering that I am not the company for which I work. That is the piece I need to figure out—how to separate myself from my work."

Carole continued, "What I am working on now is not pushing my jaded and cynical parts away. Instead, I want to recognize, acknowledge, and know that it is okay that they are there, yet still rely on my Wise One Within to keep those parts' perspectives in context. My Wise One Within can say, 'Thank you for what you are concerned about, but let's take a bit of a break and step back a moment.'"

The Wise One Within granted Carole such a sense of comfort that Carole would take walks around a field next to her home to tap into her reassuring presence more every week. Strengthening their connection helped Carole to lean more on her own sense of self, rather than waiting for someone else to give her permission to feel whole and worthy.

What is experienced in sessions like these can go beyond the words that describe them. Sometimes, when clients share out loud the messages they hear in their guided journeys, they feel self-conscious about some of the words that come through, even judging them to be cheesy or cliché. For example, the phrase, "Love yourself and give yourself a hug," if taken out of context and the emotional space, could feel empty or meaningless. However, even if simply phrased—or seemingly sweet and idyllically kind—when words like these ring true in the visualization, they can powerfully touch someone, often to the point of tears, laughter, and amazement.

Even if your inner protectors are preemptively judging your encounters, other parts of you may feel that the wisdom of the Wise One Within resonates on an important level. The wisdom you receive may be something you have heard before or that sounds picture-perfect, but if it moves you, then it is the right medicine. When you are open to it, you can understand it not as an empty catchphrase, but as a truth you can embody more and more.

You can increase your access to the guidance of your Wise One Within in many ways. Simply taking a few deep breaths and inviting its presence can be effective. Another good way to contact this fountain of inner wisdom is to write letters to and from your Wise One Within to see what messages are in store for you. Now, you will get a chance to connect to your Wise One Within through this letter-writing process.

CHAPTER 7 ACTIVITY:

Tap into Your Wise One
Within Through Letter Writing

1) WRITE TO YOUR WISE ONE WITHIN *(30 minutes)*

› Think of a challenge you are facing that you would like some guidance around. If it brings up worry, fear, or doubt, connect with those struggles or inner tensions, noticing what sensations arise and allowing them to be.

› Either by typing, writing, or audio-recording, share from the vantage point of your small self part. This can be any aspect of you who is taken over by the usual barrage of fears, hesitations, and worries. Have this smaller self ask your Wise One Within for guidance around this particular struggle, explaining the current situation in detail and welcoming support.

› When you are done, either seal the letter you wrote or close your digital document or file so that you can let insights arise as this message marinates over the next few days.

2) RECEIVE THE RESPONSE *(30 minutes)*

› About three days later, when you feel inspired to revisit the letter, take a few moments to meditate, breathe, and ground.

› Then, open the first letter mindfully. Reread it from the perspective of your Wise One Within. If it is a voice memo, play it back and hear it from a meditative open space while connected to your inner wisdom.

› Now, respond to the concerns listed in the letter from the perspective of your Wise One Within, who can offer calm, gentle, and reassuring guidance.

› Do not overthink, just feel into what words of comfort or encouragement you would give in response to the first letter. What does that worried part need to know, hear, and receive that would be supportive?

› When you have delivered the answer, you can read it back to yourself out loud or play it back and see how the response feels to you.

Tip: If you prefer to speak aloud into a recording instead of writing, when you listen back, you will be able to listen for tone of voice, speed of speech, and other factors related to the energy of your worried self and your Wise One Within.

CHAPTER 7 KEY CONCEPTS

› Part of the spiritual path can involve an unfolding process of learning lessons, making messes, and receiving blessings. Encountering the Wise One Within through parts work is one way to facilitate an experience of the beauty that this path holds.

› Your Wise One Within helps you feel *connected*—to your full self, to others, and to that which is greater than you.

› Working with parts helps you move from feeling scattered and lost to charting a course toward your North Star—a path of purpose, vitality, and alignment.

› You can best navigate toward greater clarity and joy via your Wise One Within, a presence who is loving, compassionate, warm, and magnanimous and who acts as your inner compass.

› When connected to this fountain of inner wisdom, you can access resources previously untapped and feel a resulting increase in your sense of inner alignment.

› Your Wise One Within is a space in you that can lovingly witness and hold all of your parts. It is a place you can access in yourself akin to the witnessing stance when meditating.

› Knowing, gracious, noble, and kind, the Wise One Within can help anchor you and support you, like a comforting friend. Contact with this transcendent self—or an experience of being able to view yourself through the Wise One Within's lens—tends to result in feelings of peace and harmony.

› The Wise One Within is not a future or ideal version of you but rather has always been with you and is with you now as well. You can connect to this element of your being in the form of a person, or even light, a color, or a feeling.

> As we reviewed in the last chapter, dark or troublesome parts are merely crying out for love. We cannot run from or get rid of our "negative" or unwanted parts. They are likely vulnerable or wounded parts that need healing, which can be facilitated by the Wise One Within's loving, patient, accepting, and non-judgmental embrace.

> The goal of this chapter's activity is to cultivate a stronger connection with your Wise One Within, opening to this deep well of love within and around you through letter-writing for support and guidance.

CHAPTER 8

FINDING HOME WITHIN YOURSELF

Let Wholeness Lead the Way

Wisdom tells me I am nothing.
Love tells me I am everything.
Between the two my life flows.

— NISARGADATTA MAHARAJ

Weaving together your journey thus far, this chapter will help you lay the foundation for cultivating peace within and around you. By embracing every member of your inner team, you can find a sense of home in the center of your being. From this place, you can lead and be led by the wholeness of your true nature.

By aligning with your Wise One Within as you integrate your parts, you can embody what you value most. As you move into your future, you can hone your intuition, affirm your intentions, and gain confidence in your next steps. In this way, we now end this book at the threshold of your new beginning.

ALIGN WITH THE HIGHEST AND DEEPEST VERSION OF YOURSELF

Through this journey, you have learned to embrace each of your parts' messages and needs rather than resisting or ignoring important aspects of you. The result of this work is that you become more aligned with your inner truth as you connect with all your parts and as they connect with each other.

Applying the work in this book does not mean you will have a seamless path ahead. It does mean, however, that rather than be at war with yourself, you can meet your own ambivalence with the understanding of how to work through it and find out what it is trying to teach you. By navigating your inner world with curiosity, openness, and sincerity, you can enjoy the journey more thoroughly. You will find yourself increasingly resourced to handle challenges that come your way.

At the same time, you need not strive for perfection by thinking you must be your Wise One Within at all times. Instead, the aspiration can be to live with ever-increasing authenticity—being honest with yourself and with how you share that self with the world. Having met your distinct parts, you are now familiar with the inner cooks in the kitchen and you can advance on your path from a place of internal cooperation. By tuning in to the gifts that each part has to offer, you forge a direction informed by your connection to the wholeness of your inner system. Rallying all your parts toward your greater good allows you to create the circumstances you want to bring forth as you cultivate a more cohesive way of being.

After all, a fulfilling future is one where you are connected. This includes connection to yourself, to those around you, and to something greater than you—whether that is through a spiritual path or faith, the natural world, or a cause that will improve your community. The clarity, confidence, peace, and joy you seek are unleashed as byproducts of the authenticity that emerges from honoring your whole self.

HOME WITHIN YOU

We create many different types of homes. By working with your parts, you create a home in your own being comprised of your inner community. When you begin to relax into this home you have been seeking, you feel increasingly secure, cherished, and connected from the inside out. Remember, you cannot bypass or banish parts. Rather, make sure to attend to them with love. Pay attention, listen, and allow them to transform. Commit to becoming like a guest house where all your parts are welcome and held.

Too often, our own illusion of urgency suffocates the very thing it is trying to attain. In contrast, coming home to yourself means knowing that you are capable and wise enough to meet whatever arises. It also means releasing attachment to your own specific timelines or ideas of how things should look in favor of listening to what is trying to come to you and through you. Relying on the home within you means trusting in your capacity to learn, grow, rise, let go, or hold on, as necessary.

When you work with your parts and let them teach you, there is less stress about getting more or becoming better. The need to self-improve diminishes because you understand that you are already whole and that learning is a lifelong process. The emphasis instead becomes on approaching yourself, your parts, and others with compassion, enabling greater harmony within and around you. Your self-acceptance will foster transformation and growth, and inspire your self-expression, even if the one you are first expressing yourself to is you!

Instead of grasping at external straws, can you find rest through cultivating your inner hearth? Can you feel warmed by the fire of your own inherent worth? Do you dare trust enough to dwell there? As you continue working with your parts and welcoming them all home, you are invited to reside in this space. When you inevitably veer off track, remember to bring yourself back, returning home again and again.

VISION:
DESIGNING THE LIFE YOU DESIRE

By working with your parts, you become the author of your own story, aligning with a vision that inspires you. Connecting with this vision helps you steer the ship of your life toward that which gives you purpose, direction, and meaning.

Our lives consist of what we create through intention and action, as well as how we meet experiences that are out of our control. Sometimes, our own grand plans are actually too limited and can constrict what wants to come forth. It is much more rewarding to co-create with the unexpected turns, allowing our lives themselves to guide us. Life can be seen as a collaborative dance between what we desire and design and how well we respond, listen to, and follow what beckons us to learn and grow.

When forming your vision, it may be tempting to lead with the question, "What do I want?" However, this question can invoke a blank stare at best and panic at worst. Different parts of you may have different reactions to this question and battle over the answer. Asking ourselves what we want in life, relationships, and work is important, but this inquiry mostly speaks to just what we *think* we want. It may evoke what we imagine is good for us based on our current understanding and might send us chasing after an empty desire. This question is laden with the assumption that if only we knew what we wanted, we would be able to get it. However, often those impulses are mistaken, informed by only one part of us.

When we come from a compassionate and curious perspective that honors all our parts, we might ask this question differently. Instead of probing with, "What do I *want?*", we reframe the inquiry by asking, "What is *important* to me?" or "What *matters* to me?" These related questions are not about obtaining far away desires or *adding* something on that is "out there." Instead, they are more about *letting go* and paring down to what you care about most. The answers to these inquiries only come after we have released what is irrelevant and distracting. Our response to what matters to us may *include* what we desire, yet it also makes space for what is most essential. By asking what is important to us, we actually invoke the idea of starting from where we are and organically expanding outward from that core place. We can see that our next steps are built into where we are standing. Thus, inquiring about what matters most allows us to receive what is already here and then welcome the conditions that nurture our values as we move towards what is next.

CONFIDENCE IN YOUR NEXT STEPS

One of the properties scientifically used to determine what constitutes life is *movement*. This quality applies to our inner life just as much as to our bodies. When we move through our emotions internally, we express their vitality. When we move through our days with all our parts on board, rather than staying stuck in resistance or avoidance, we gain more confidence by virtue of showing up.

The Latin root of the word confidence, *fid*, means "to trust." Thus, confidence is not merely self-agency, a requirement to do it yourself, or an ungrounded sense of merely plowing onward. It involves faith—in yourself, in all your parts, and in the world you inhabit. Deep confidence comes from trusting your inner compass so that you can let go enough to be led and feel assured enough to take inspired action.

Confidence is thus connected to trusting our intuition. This intuition is the ability to tap into what we already know but have been hiding from ourselves. When we are honest with ourselves and trust in our wholeness, we can rally our inner troops in a meaningful direction.

This is much more fulfilling than being motivated by superficial desires, which usually feel empty, even if attained.

Having confidence does not mean you have everything figured out. Your life will always present unknowns—things to explore that inspire or challenge you. The richness of life lies in how you meet these unknowns. Let the resulting questions be fodder for self-inquiry. It is not about your parts themselves, or the weeds or flowers in the garden of your life, so much as it is about how you relate to all those things.

—

Now, in Donna's story, we will see how tapping into her intuition and harmonizing a medley of parts helped her make choices from her whole unified self. She crafted a guiding vision for herself so she could remain aligned with her true direction.

DONNA'S TRUTH:
TUNING INTO INTUITION

Donna had worked extensively in the technology field and had interviews with several large companies lined up, but she was feeling called in a different direction. However, she was not sure she could leave her secure life behind and trust herself to pivot. You may relate with having an underlying desire for something, yet not giving yourself permission to admit it, pursue it, or, better yet, receive it.

Donna knew that she felt excited about having a bigger and more aligned vision to work toward. But when she tuned in, she also saw major fears keeping her stuck. She was afraid of not living up to her potential, of being in yet another toxic work environment that would rob her of her gifts, and of never truly belonging. She sought to cultivate compassion for herself in the process of exploring a new career path.

In a guided visualization session, I introduced the presence of the Wise One Within. Donna initially said it was hard to conjure up a concrete image of what she called her Higher Self. As Donna began to feel more grounded, her Higher Self started to materialize.

Donna: She is a woman of the elements. She honors fire, earth, water, and air. She radiates passion. She does not sacrifice her fire for anything. She does not let it control her, but it is very important. The fire is in her heart and soul, and she moves by that compass with a life-giving spirit.

Donna became more connected with this Higher Self and came up to stand right beside her, holding hands.

Donna: (tears arising) She tells me it's okay, and I feel very calm through her. I can feel her wisdom help my fire. She reignites it without having it blow everywhere. She rekindles it in a healthy way. . . . Wow, this is so powerful!

Donna then gave her Higher Self a warm hug, feeling permission to soften.

Donna: The message my Higher Self is giving me is, "You do not have to fight so hard within yourself."

Then, we introduced Donna's fear of making a big change into this scene.

Donna: My fear part is sort of like a creature from the movie Monsters, Inc. It has big eyes and is scrunched over like a greyish blob. It is not scary, though. It is cowering like Gollum from *The Lord of the Rings*. It is small.

Jeanine: This creature seems to have been in the driver's seat lately. What is its name?

Donna: The Fearful Blob.

The Higher Self welcomes the Fearful Blob.

Donna: In the presence of my Higher Self, the blob suddenly turns into light and is no longer grey. I am realizing that the blob is kind of like a cowering pet. But when my Higher Self touches it, it becomes like an excited puppy. It is like my younger self, whom I want to regain. My younger self was curious and joyous, just like an eager puppy.

The Fearful Blob turned Puppy then offers Donna a doggie bag.

Jeanine: What is in this doggie bag?

Donna: It is almost like a piece of my heart returned to me!

Jeanine: Which piece?

Donna: Something very core and very deep. It looks like just a piece, but really it's a seed. It is a seed that gets planted, strengthens, and blossoms.

Jeanine: How do you feel as this seed begins to take root?

Donna: My heart is full and blossoming. And I am in this field now with flowers and sunlight and green! I feel grounded and free. The freedom comes from being rooted. I feel radiant from my chest up to my head. My Puppy Self is running around, chasing butterflies. My Higher Self is standing next to her and absorbing the beauty with her hand on my back.

Jeanine: What do you desire from this space?

Donna: I desire to be soft and to feel held. I desire support and community with people who are also walking this earth with a similar intention. I desire to feel fully and to light a fire in other people too. The fire is really my instrument, and I want to honor my fire not only by using it but by feeding it. I desire to connect with people who recognize and honor my fire and are open to it. The fire is ultimately like a campfire. People are drawn to it and surrounding it, connecting with others around it, telling stories around it. We need warmth; we are nourished by warmth. I see other women coming around and feeling emboldened by it. I just desire to be me!

Jeanine: From this place, complete the phrase, "I am . . . "

Donna: *(with confidence)* I am content and passionate. I am water and fire. I am the elements. I am soft and strong. I am flexible and powerful. I am rooted and free. I am in control but also an agent of the universe. I can find myself, but I'm also open to being found. I am resting. I'm absorbing. I just am! And, it feels so right.

Donna: *(emerging from the visualization)* That was cathartic. It is like after the winter, this was the spring rain. I needed this because it means I am not numbing myself anymore. Rather, I am re-watering myself and being open to possibility.

After integrating those newfound desires and affirmations, Donna began to lead her life from a new place within herself. She consulted her intuition for daily choices like what to eat that would feel most nourishing, and for bigger decisions, like what to do for her next career step. Donna ended up continuing to work in the technology industry part-time in a way that felt more aligned. She felt more fulfilled with that line of work while enjoying the flexibility and freedom to explore her outlets for creative and healing paths.

In addition, she felt compelled to strengthen her creative and artistic side, shining fully in her work as a performance artist. She eventually crafted a one-woman show, bringing her full voice to the stage and making art where she could channel some of her raw experiences and hit a chord with audiences.

Donna shared, "More than anything, I learned to trust my intuition, and I've been deepening my relationship with it ever since. Now, I can let things unfold and feel like I am in a flow rather than stuck in mental consternation." For Donna, learning to lean on her intuition, rather than just rational intellect, was a game-changer.

Speaking to her a year later, she reflected on her new relationship with her intuition and wholeness. Donna shared, "Meeting my parts in the guided visualizations was so helpful. Some people think intuition is just amorphous or at best a 'gut feeling' but working with my parts made it feel concrete. Now, when I hear my inner child pipe up, I know I need soothing. Or, if I feel the absence of the Inner Muse too much, I know I need to nurture her and bring her out more. Since I drew them, visualized them, and brought them to life, I am more aware of these parts of myself. Now, I have integrated them so much since our work together that they just flow naturally. I especially love tuning in to the voice of the Higher Self. She comes from such a grounded, trusting, and peaceful place. Now I do not doubt my intuition anymore. Of course, fear comes along with any kind of change, but I trust my intuition now and am choosing to follow it."

To crystallize her experience with her parts, Donna made a watercolor depicting a cluster of resourced parts (Inner Muse, Higher Self, and Core Self) in a natural setting after meeting them through a guided meditation journey. Then, she made a vision board with the aspects of her most resourced selves to keep them close to mind. She sketched a committee of her empowered selves that she envisioned nurturing and growing into, including Inner Genius, Pushing Bounds, and Thriving Woman.

As you can see with Donna's story, connecting with your parts and integrating them can help you commit to a future vision that inspires you, while remaining flexible to how that vision might take shape.

RECEIVING THE GIFTS OF YOUR LIFE

When you tend to all of your parts with love, you do not banish core aspects of yourself to live in the shadows. You can welcome the gifts that your parts have to offer and be more receptive to the gifts of life around you.

Fear can overrun our unintegrated parts. These parts may be obsessed with a sense of not having or being enough. They may believe that the only way to fulfill their needs is to make demands on others.

However, as you work with parts, you come to learn that this desperate approach actually deprives you of what you desire: wholeness. You cannot have your hands both clenched and open at the same time. You can never receive what you try to take—and you will never be able to give what you have not fully received.

By trying to take something, you rob others of the gift of freely and generously giving from the heart. At the same time, you also rob yourself of the gift of letting things come to you and being able to open your arms to them.

Receiving anything fully takes appreciation. Without appreciation, anything you do not have or have not accepted (even if you technically physically "have" it) will be something you feel that you are lacking, and thus are unable to share.

AFFIRMING YOUR FUTURE

In one drop of water are found all the secrets of all the oceans;
in one aspect of You are found all the aspects of existence.

— KHALIL GIBRAN

To honor the gifts of your parts is to be open to the gifts of your life. You open to the wisdom, creativity, compassion, and joy within your true self. You open to seeing others more clearly as well, separate from you in their own humanity instead of players to assuage feelings of emptiness or reassure you. By honoring their unique experience, you give others the gift of loving them without expectation or distortion. You open to life's wonders which remind you that you are held and loved just as you are.

Only by starting from the premise of love can any of your parts shift and truly grow, expand, and deepen. By facilitating a connection to your Wise One Within, you can become grateful for the spark of divinity in each part. From that place, you are whole.

Living with this sense of love for yourself and others gives you the courage, curiosity, and assurance to face what comes your way with grace. It allows you to trust in your own agency and live in your own truth.

As we end this journey together, ask yourself: What can you let go of and leave behind? What do you want to carry with you and cultivate? What seeds are you planting?

WHAT WILL
YOU AFFIRM?

When you are aligned with your true self, you can cultivate gratitude for what is coming and feel as if it were true now using affirmations. Affirmations are statements that articulate a truth as a reminder of what is possible and also what is already here.

In creating your desired future, declaring an intention in an "I AM" statement can be helpful, because it affirms that at least the seeds of what you want are present in your desire for it. So, if you are feeling you want more contentment, you could say or write down, "I am Peaceful" or "I am Serene." Sometimes, this is referred to as "acting as-if." We embody what we desire on the level of feeling before seeing evidence of it in our lives. Our faith starts to give us eyes to see the beginnings of what we desire and fan the flames of its unfolding.

When you affirm who you are now and who you are becoming, you can embody your values and live into them. Turning an intention into a present-tense statement that you affirm can be helpful. It must feel true enough that you feel the seed of it in you already so you do not provoke parts who will say, "Yeah, right, that is not even close!"

What are you affirming on a daily basis? Are you encouraging your fears or nurturing your powerful aspirations? As the saying goes, "Worry is praying for what you don't want to happen." When we give our fear attention, we are giving it our most valuable resource—our time!

We create our world with our words. Our language, both internally and externally, creates our story. If we cultivate who we are today and who we are becoming, what we see outside ourselves will shift too. As Anaïs Nin says, "We see the world not as it is, but as we are."

Via your intention, set your tone for each activity in your day. This can help you to reframe, remember, and stand in the leadership stance of the Wise One Within. Affirm who you are now through acceptance. Affirm who you are becoming by allowing yourself room to evolve. Harmonize with all your parts to allow your whole self to lead the way.

—

Now, we will take a look at an example of how Eric used the power of connecting with his parts to affirm what was most important to him— in life and love. Through connecting with his Wise One Within, Eric began to create the future he imagined for himself.

ERIC'S STORY:
ENVISIONING THE EMERGING FUTURE

As a talented entrepreneur, photographer, and app developer, Eric was enjoying success in his career when we started working together. However, he wanted to experience the same satisfaction in his personal life, too—especially romantically. Eric had gone through a recent break-up but, after several months, he felt ready to start dating again.

We began our session with a short centering meditation, and I asked Eric to set his intention for the work.

Eric: My intention is to identify what I want in an open and authentic way and to listen to my intuition. I seek space and permission to want what I want and to feel what I feel.

Jeanine: What is the biggest obstacle to this intention?

Eric: My tendency to tap into what others want and match them, even if it doesn't feel good or right to me. Also, my focus on pleasing whomever I am partnered with and accommodating their needs or desires. I tend to become someone else in my attempt to hold on to them.

We then explored some of the main qualities he wanted in a partner, which included: an intellectual match, someone to share and amplify his experience of life with, and a woman who shares her unique gifts with the world.

Jeanine: Who would *you* be in this ideal relationship?

Eric: I would help her achieve whatever she is after, using my resources to give and to support. I would like to provide fun experiences, dates, and trips and create lasting memories. I would be her rock through whatever comes up for her, supporting her passions in a healthy way.

Jeanine: And how do you want to *feel* in this relationship?

Eric: I want to feel seen, heard, received, challenged, supported, and loved. I want to share in the process of discovery as we both witness the unfolding of one another.

Jeanine: Is there anything else you are longing for?

Eric: Yes—closeness, intimacy, and connection through openness and vulnerability.

Pause.

Eric: As I say that, I realize I am terrified I will not be able to find what I am looking for. Or that if I find it, I may feel undeserving and be afraid to lose it. In the past, I have tried to become who I thought my partner wanted me to be, at the expense of my own self-expression. At the same time, what I truly want is to eventually get married and have kids. I am not in a hurry unless I feel an alignment, then I could be! I'm okay to date first and keep being true to myself regarding the next steps.

Employing guided visualization, we began an inner journey. I first invited Eric's Wise One Within onto the figurative field, whom we referred to as his Higher Self. Eric closed his eyes as he imagined the scene.

Eric: My Higher Self is older, in his 40s, sturdy, tall, and smiling. He is walking smoothly and slowly, confidently. He carries inner comfort. He is not wound up; he exudes kindness and love, cherishing life.

Jeanine: If this Higher Self had a scroll with a message on it, what would it say?

Eric: It would say, "I could tell you all the secrets, but it is a lot more fun discovering them. Just know to trust yourself and to follow the path to which you are drawn. Trust your intuition and test your assumptions on the path to a great life."

Eric saw himself tuck the scroll away into a pocket near his heart.

Next, Eric's Core Self entered, his pure inner child. This figure appeared as a 4-year-old boy, wearing a small cap and dressed in a conductor's outfit.

Eric: He is smiling so big that his cheeks are red! I loved trains as a kid, so it's funny that I see my Core Self riding in on a little green train with red trimmings. His energy is squirmy and excited.

Jeanine: If this Core Self had a gift for you, what would he offer to you now?

Eric: He gives me a pocket watch that is both nice and old looking. He's actually curious about it, saying, "Hey, how cool is this? Look, it's for you!"

Eric observed the texture and design of the old pocket watch. He felt humbled that though the child loved this object, he was willing to offer it to Eric.

Eric: *(filled with appreciation)* What a gift!

Jeanine: What happens next?

Eric: I pop the watch open. *(pauses)* Inside it, there's an old grandfather clock dial, and on the inside cover, there is an inscription. Wow. It says, "Love what you love, with all that you are."

Eric felt moved by these words and proceeded to clip the chain of this watch to his button-down shirt. With the chain across his chest, he slipped the watch into his pocket.

Upon coming back from this inner creative and imaginative space, Eric reported that he felt safe exploring these spaces within himself and that the messages he received were priceless.

He was so moved by this encounter with these parts of himself that he had a custom replica made of the token his Core Self gave him.

Eric crafted a symbolic object to bring to life the message from his Core Self.

Fast forward to a few years later: Eric is now joyfully married with a child, and another on the way!

Like Eric, some people are so impacted by the symbolism they experience when interacting with their parts that they find an object in the physical world as a reminder of the transformation that occurred.

CHAPTER 8 ACTIVITIES:

Align with Who You Are Becoming

1) **REFLECTION PROMPTS** *(1 hour)*

› Who are you when you are aligned, harmonious, and at your fullest?

› What activities bring these qualities out in you most readily?

› If you became who you most want to be and embraced living your most authentic and expressed life, what more would you have to give?

› Your calling is calling! What are you feeling summoned toward internally or externally? What is in the way of following that call? What is there to lose in resisting it? What is there to gain in saying "Yes!"?

› What makes you come alive? Where have you found joy in the past? What brings you joy these days? Is there anything in the way of feeling that joy? What activities, actions, thoughts, habits, or people in your life support that aliveness?

› What visions seem far into the future? Can you begin to see your underlying need or desire as seeds of that vision and start to cultivate them, starting right here? What would the next steps be?

› What is most important to you now? What matters? What are your core needs, desires, and values?

2) TOKEN REMINDER *(45 minutes)*

› Select a physical object to have on your person, or on a nightstand or altar at home, to help crystallize your connection to the Wise One Within or any resourced parts that inspire you.

› If you like, you can create a ritual to go along with the use of your object. For example, light a candle and meditate with the object nearby. Or, ring a singing bowl three times, taking three deep breaths, or create a mantra to recite while holding it in your hand.

3) WHOLENESS AFFIRMATIONS *(45 minutes)*

Read aloud the following pages with some examples of Affirmations for Wholeness, then write 5-10 of your own. You can craft these from several vantage points: from a specific part in its valuable role, from the perspective of your Wise One Within, or from the state of wholeness that includes all your parts.

Starting with something that feels true and which you would like to continue to imbue with energy and cultivate, begin each sentence with phrases such as:

› I am . . .

› I know . . .

› I affirm . . .

› I trust . . .

› I believe . . .

› I commit to . . .

AFFIRMATIONS
FOR WHOLENESS

› I know myself as both one and many at the same time.

› I welcome whatever parts of me arise today. I make a place for each of them at the table of my Self.

› I trust that all parts of me are inherently valuable and want my highest good.

› I know that through the light of my awareness and depth of my understanding, all parts of me have a chance to share their unique wisdom.

› I believe that the unwanted parts of me are thirsty for love and that their cries are the only way they know how to get it. I vow to love these shadowy parts so they feel held, cared for, seen, known, appreciated, and relaxed.

› I appreciate my parts for being with me and doing the best they know how to keep me safe and true. When any part feels full of fear, doubt, or judgment, I tune in to their particular needs and find new paths to meet those precious needs.

› I acknowledge the parts at play in those around me and hold their deepest needs and truest desires with as much care as I do my own.

› I acknowledge the beauty, goodness, joy, creativity, and love in my life, expanding their presence with my attention and care.

› I commit to embodying the values dearest to me and to becoming a living expression of what matters most to me to contribute to making this world more loving, kind, compassionate, and peaceful.

› I am wise and I let myself be led from the truth of my inner knowing.

› I trust my Wise One Within to move, inspire, and guide me. In turn, I am open to listening and following that guidance.

› I am grateful. I appreciate all parts of my being and all the lessons and experiences that shape my becoming.

› I am compassionate and I approach myself and others with kindness, care, and love.

CHAPTER 8 KEY CONCEPTS

› There is wisdom within all your parts. It can be healing to listen to your parts and connect with their intentions.

› You can find home within when you align yourself with the value of all your parts and integrate them into the truth of who you are.

› The clarity, confidence, peace, and joy you seek all follow from honoring the authenticity of your whole self.

› Clarifying your vision can support you to build on your strengths, find meaning and purpose, and share your gifts.

› It can be helpful to have written affirmations of the values you want to embody or the intentions you want to live into. These words can encourage and inspire you.

› Carry a symbolic object with you to anchor yourself to your Wise One Within or an inspiring part of you as a reminder of your wholeness and this journey.

› To have confidence in your next steps, you can: cultivate faith in yourself, trust in those around you, and rely on something greater that moves you.

› To determine your next steps, ask, "What matters to me?" instead of, "What do I want?" This reframe will steer you in the direction of your deepest aspirations and core values, while allowing you to begin where you are.

CONCLUSION

Thank you for taking this journey with me. I hope this book has helped you better understand and accept all of who you are so that you can make clear and aligned choices moving forward.

You do not need to fear that the sense of peace, empowerment, or inspiration you might begin to feel will disappear. Rather, working with your parts is a lifestyle—a way of being that can be lived into and lived out.

In his book *The Prophet*, Khalil Gibran says, "Say not, 'I have found the truth,' but rather, 'I have found a truth.'" Your larger truth is not a tale that tells itself all at once in an ultimate way. Instead, it is woven by a composite of smaller daily insights, knowings, and realizations that are gleaned and compounded day-by-day.

CONTINUING TO
WORK WITH PARTS

Continuing to work with your parts can create shifts externally that begin within. As you take what you have learned and experienced in this book, it will help to hold expectations lightly, allow yourself to be led, and enjoy the continued exploration. This work is not meant to be a peak experience so much as a way of navigating your inner terrain and traversing it with more grace.

Like most things, this work is a practice. Motivational speaker Zig Ziglar once said, "People often say that motivation doesn't last. Well, neither does bathing, that's why we recommend it daily." Let yourself be in the process as a work in progress. After investing so much dedicated effort so far, remember to also enjoy and celebrate the fruits of your labor—the surprising, creative, and rewarding results that come from nurturing your parts and deepening your relationship with them.

As you integrate this work and take it off the page and into your days, you can cultivate a sustained awareness of what parts live within you. You can choose to continue showing up for your parts, knowing they, in turn, will show up for you. This book offers a toolkit for meeting your inner aspects and an approach for welcoming their messages. You can now revisit any of the activities and concepts, putting them to use in any new circumstance that calls for self-acceptance, clarity, or a renewal of confidence sourced from your full self.

Staying in touch with your parts will allow you to deepen your connection with your truth, freedom, and joy. You may also want to relate with your parts in the day-to-day, making it a habit to tune in to their needs and messages. For example, you could start reading something inspirational for 20 minutes daily to satisfy a part like Lifelong Learner Lenny. You could wear a favorite accessory without waiting for a special occasion to express a Muse. Or, you might visit an intriguing place and try a new activity to activate a part like Adventurous Al.

When you want to feel the integration of all your parts, give yourself permission to pause, sit, and be with whatever arises within you. Observe yourself and your surroundings free of expectations or agenda. Committing to any of these aligned action steps in your external reality will help your parts feel valued and honored by your attention and your actions.

WORKING WITH
EXTERNAL GUIDES

This book focuses on connecting with your parts on your own, but it can be helpful to have a therapist, coach, or knowledgeable partner as a guide. In therapy, the most effective element is the relationship between the therapist and the patient (called the "therapeutic alliance"). I would venture that this works in the case of coaching too, between practitioner and client. A Swedish proverb states, "Joy shared is doubled, and grief shared is halved." Someone skilled, deeply attentive, and curious can help to hold the emotions that arise, be they joyful or sorrowful. Thus, the relationship between you and your guide in parts work can be extra special because you have someone knowledgeable and kind to support you.

The client's own inner resources and, if there is a guide, the coach's or therapist's approach act as two key aspects of this energetic container. When we feel held, it allows us to go deep within. In coaching, this rapport is built between the practitioner and the client as well as all their parts. If you do choose to work with a guide, it is still important to rely on your center through the process as, ultimately, your development and growth is up to you.

GUIDED VISUALIZATION

Parts work can happen in many forms. In this book, we have covered ways you can connect to them on your own. When I work with parts during coaching sessions, I often employ a guided meditation process that I call a "Co-Created Visualization Journey." This experience is co-created because, though I offer structure, guidance, and direction to the journey, the client is doing the sacred work of delving into their own psychic world, dictating what they both see and feel as they encounter different parts. I ask guiding questions, and the client responds with decisions that lead the unfolding narrative, much like a "choose your own adventure" novel. I, in turn, take cues from what is arising in their experience.

Clients have compared these guided visualizations to a trance-like state or a lucid dream. The inner journey can feel like entering a symbolic realm where images and situations present themselves vividly, and one is both watching this "movie" unfold while also co-directing it on the spot. The immersive process requires both focus and receptivity to allow what emerges to evoke transformation.

If you would like to explore working with your parts in this way, Guided Visualization Journey tracks are available on my website: **jeaninecerundolo.com/meditations**

THE WORLD HAS A HOLE
IN THE SHAPE OF YOUR GIFT

What you create, do, say, and share is all valuable and can contribute to others in such a meaningful way. Yet, one of the most comforting things to discover is that your unique youness is what inspires each of those actions or offerings. You are the one who is irreplaceable. Your voice has a place and you deserve to claim it. You get to take up space—you, and all your beautiful parts.

This world has a hole in the shape of your gift—and the gift you have to give is *you*. So much of the process of learning to love yourself actually lies in letting go of all the stories, pains, and distorted beliefs that are in the way of revealing the true you. We are like diamonds that got dusty over time, having been tucked away. When you recognize the gem that you are, and the value that you offer by simply being yourself, then you can dust off the diamond and reveal the beauty that has always been there. Just as a diamond cannot be scratched, the inherent value that you have cannot be marred, only hidden.

THE GIFTS YOU RECEIVE
ARE NOW YOURS TO GIVE

Reflect on how you have grown so far through working with your parts. These learnings expand when you share the essence of your journey with others. By aligning with this deeper place that houses the *true you*, you benefit not just yourself but anyone you interact with or can impact.

Whatever gifts you have received are actually a gift for others too. What you have gained, learned, and become is meant to be shared—in what you do, but also through who and how you are.

This poem by the mystic Persian poet Hafiz (translated by Daniel Ladinksy) offers us an invitation to shift from yearning and longing to warmth and belonging:

WITH THAT MOON LANGUAGE

Admit something:

Everyone you see, you say to them, "Love me."
Of course you do not do this out loud, otherwise
someone would call the cops.

Still, though, think about this, this great pull in us to connect.

Why not become the one who lives with a
full moon in each eye that is
always saying,

with that sweet moon language,
what every other eye in
this world is
dying to
hear?

—

When you align with your own wholeness, then you will not have to force yourself to give resentfully out of obligation nor to try to gain anything in return. Rather, you can share because your cup runs over, naturally expanding what is inside you. When you practice being aligned and free, you will not spend so much time battling yourself. You will have freedom, joy, and clarity that enables you to be empowered and to serve.

As we love ourselves more deeply, we can give and receive love in turn. We can care for others with a generous heart, helping their parts feel loved as well. Imagine how the world could be if we did this as a collective!

Just as we have parts that we are the sum of, we can think of ourselves as a part of the sum of the world around us. Like each cell in the human body has its unique function, we are each like a cell in the body of humanity. Our vibrancy and participation impact the whole.

Consider what is possible once you, your Wise One Within, and all your parts begin to work in tandem as a team. How does this wholeness impact your life, your loved ones, and the world around you?

May you enjoy the grace of being all of who you are and savor the gift of sharing your light in a way that feels aligned, connected, and true.

REFERENCES

Holmes, T., Holmes, L., & Eckstein, S. (2007). *Parts work: An illustrated guide to your inner life.* Kalamazoo, MI: Winged Heart Press.

Rosenberg, M. B. (2003). *Nonviolent communication: A language of life.* Encinitas, CA: PuddleDancer Press.

RELATED TOPICS

Active Imagination, Archetypes, and Complexes (Carl Jung)

Psychosynthesis (Roberto Assagioli)

Gestalt Therapy (Frederick & Laura Perls)

Sub-Personalities (Eric Rowan)

Ego State Therapy (Eric Bernes)

Voice Dialogue (Stone & Stone)

Psychodrama (Jacob Moreno)

RESOURCES FOR FURTHER STUDY

Internal Family Systems Therapy developed by Richard Schwartz:

https://ifs-institute.com/

Greater than the Sum of Our Parts: Discovering Your True Self Through Internal Family Systems Therapy, by Richard Schwartz (Sounds True, 2018)

Internal Family Systems Therapy, Second Edition, by Richard C. Schwartz, and Martha Sweezy (The Guilford Press, 2019)

Self-Therapy, by Jay Earley (Pattern System Books, 2010)

SoulCollage® international website: www.soulcollage.com

SoulCollage® Evolving, by Seena B. Frost

Recovery of Your Inner Child: The Highly Acclaimed Method for Liberating Your Inner Self, by Lucia Capacchione (Touchstone, 1991)

Inner Bonding: Becoming a Loving Adult to Your Inner Child, by Margaret Paul (HarperOne, 1992)

The Power of Focusing: A Practical Guide to Emotional Self-Healing, by Ann Weiser Cornell (New Harbinger Publications, 1996)

SUPPLEMENTAL MATERIALS

Visit **jeaninecerundolo.com/meditations** for more information and as well as guided tracks related to this work.

ABOUT THE AUTHOR

JEANINE CERUNDOLO is a holistic life coach who has worked to support thousands of people across the world in living their most authentic and connected lives. She devotes herself to writing, coaching, and group facilitation, offering transformational tools for personal and professional development.

Jeanine's clients are simultaneous go-getters and go-givers whose inner growth and outward contributions help make their communities thrive. Jeanine holds a master's degree in Clinical Psychology from Columbia University. She loves to help others to deepen the love and creative expression in their lives. In this book, she shares a decade of personal and professional experience to support readers in accessing the wisdom, compassion, and confidence within.

Learn more about Jeanine and her latest offerings at:
jeaninecerundolo.com

GRATITUDE

*Every blade of grass has an angel that bends over
it and whispers, 'Grow! Grow!'*

— TALMUD

Much appreciation and love to the many people who have helped both myself and this book to grow, especially:

All the Indiegogo contributors (friends near and far): who backed this project before it was birthed, believed in it, and shared it.

Abuela: who led the way with her own journey as a writer, teaching me that the pen has as much power to give to the author as it offers to the reader, and who helped to edit this work, in her third language!

Abuelo: who taught me there can be a difference between your work and your vocation, but that it is never too late to honor your calling.

Author Support Group: Smiley Poswolsky and his incubator group who helped this book progress through writing tools and accountability.

Beta Readers: Jessye Chalmers, Lauren Cap, and Sydney Doolittle who gave the manuscript their fresh perspective and useful feedback.

Christine Diven: whose immense thoughtfulness and care helped to catch the little things that make a big difference.

Clients: All the beautiful souls I have had the honor of working with including those who graciously gave me their blessing to share their stories in this book.

Dad: who emphasizes the practical things while supporting me in paving my own path toward happiness on my terms.

Ellie: who has consistently believed in what my heart had to share, and for featuring this work on her podcast!

Grandma: who since seeing me write from age 8 said knowingly: "you're going to write a book like Harry Potter one day" ;-)

Grandpa: who showed me the way when I was lost, and whose memory continues to teach me to love myself as graciously and generously as he did.

Hafeez: who has nurtured this book, helping to get it into the hands and hearts of those who would appreciate its message.

Katie Asmus: whose mentorship and care has helped me cultivate my voice and grow personally, professionally, emotionally, and spiritually.

Lauren Libera: who went through the manuscript with a fine-tooth comb and whose support through thick and thin made the journey more rewarding.

Madeline Blue Schussel: whose thorough and meticulous developmental edits made the process of getting particular with the details more fun!

Michael: whose devotion to following his bliss has shined bright and illustrated how we can make our aspirations come true.

Mike and Louise: whose being in my corner has made every adventure, accomplishment, and learning into a worthwhile ride with the best companionship.

Mom: who emphasizes the importance of the beautiful things in life: poetry, art, service, and community, and who told me there was a difference between having an idea and doing something about it.

Nicole: whose being here as her has always been more than enough and who has taught me much about human love and unconditional love.

Nora Martin Cooley: who broke this book down so I could build it back up again, and whose constructive edits shepherded a new version of this work.

Richard Schwartz: whose dedication to developing and sharing the IFS model has transformed lives in profound ways, and whose seminal work helped me deepen my understanding and practice of working with parts.

Tom: whose depth and philosophical eye meaningfully shaped these pages, and who ingrained in me that it takes daily action, commitment, and devotion to bring seeds of potential into their aliveness.

To everyone else whose example, wisdom, insights, encouragement, and support helped catalyze this long-time dream into fruition:

You give me roots and wings.

Thank you!

Made in the USA
Columbia, SC
01 September 2021